Change Your Words Change Your Future

Change Your Words Change Your Future

Understanding the Incredible Power
and Impact of Your Words

JULIE THOMAS

Library of Congress Control Number: 2019920371
ISBN: 978-1-7343828-0-8 (Paperback);
ISBN: 978-1-7343828-1-5 (ebook)
Interior design: Old Mate Media

This book is dedicated to my Father

My Dad's love, humbleness, commitment to God's word, and gentle spirit is what made me the woman I am today. Dad, you have taught me so much through your life. I know you were so happy when I told you about this book. This is a dream you always wanted for yourself. Even though you have passed, I write this book for you. I love you, Dad.

To My Husband

Even though your life here on earth was short, you always encouraged and believed in me. You had a kind and gentle spirit and I pray that you are walking on the streets of gold. We miss you.

To My Mom & Family

Thank you for supporting me and always being there for me. Your love, support, and prayers will be with me forever and I am so thankful to God to have you all in my life.

CONTENTS

INTRODUCTION

God has amazing things in store for you, and He wants you to accomplish the desires He has placed within you to your fullest potential! We have a God that can do the impossible, a God that can change and transform your life and help you to be everything that you were meant to be!

What we say about ourselves, others, and those around us matters, and God gives us detailed instructions on how we can make the best of our lives. He has given us the ability to use words that are not just mere words, but rather words that can build others up and in return glorify His name. The Bible says, "Do not let any unwholesome talk come out of your mouths, but only what helps build others up according to their needs, that it may benefit those who listen" (Ephesians 4:29 NIV). When you help to meet the needs of others around you, you will begin to feel joy bubble out of you.

Every time we speak words of love, joy, peace, hope, and God's greatness we are planting seeds that will take root, and bring us into a brighter future. We all want a brighter future. To reach our highest potential, however, our future is shaped by what we say and what we declare. You have the power to change your future just by what you say and how you see your situation. When you wake up in the morning, start by coming into agreement with what God says in His word. You can start by saying, "this is the day that the Lord has made, I am going to rejoice and be glad in it!" (Psalms 118: 24). No matter what comes your way, have your mind made up that it is still going to be a good day. It is up to us to determine in advance the kind of day that we will have.

The same is true when it comes to your destiny. Whichever direction you want your life to go toward, decide to speak in the direction that you seek. It is impossible to speak defeat and expect victory, or speak words of not having enough and expect to live in abundance. Speaking the opposite of what you want in your life is not going to get you to your destination. You must speak in the direction that you seek. Whatever seed you plant is what you will reap. Decide to make a change and come into agreement with what God says you can have and what He says you can do, which is found in His word.

In this book, you will discover how your words have tremendous power and can affect the direction of your life and impact you in ways that can be life changing. These changes will be seen by all those you come in contact with, and your life will become a testimony of God's greatness and power that is at work within you. Every time you open your mouth you have the power to uplift, bring down, and in various ways impact your own life and the lives of those around you. We serve an incredible God who came to give us "life and the ability to live more abundantly" (John 10:10 ESV). However, this life can only begin when you come into agreement with His instructions and plan for your life. Are you ready to begin that new life? If so, here we go!

SECTION I

THE INCREDIBLE POWER THAT IS WITHIN YOU

CHAPTER 1

Your Words Have Power

Our words have incredible power and can impact every area of our lives. We use words every day, from the time we wake up to the time we go to bed. God has given us a mouth and a tongue over which we are in complete control. This is a big responsibility, yet it is a wonderful thing that God has given us, if we choose to use it wisely. Words are so powerful that they can bring joy or bring sadness to the one who listens to them. We can use them to bless someone, or we can use them to curse someone, but the choice is ours.

Proverbs 11:17 says, "Your soul is nourished when you are kind, but destruction can occur when you are cruel." As humans, we just feel better when we can put a smile on someone's face. Have you ever noticed that when you say something kind, it makes you feel good, versus if you say something negative it makes you feel worse? For example, if you have ever been a parent or a kid yourself, then you know how your parents spoke to you. What they said could either bring a smile to your face or a frown. We all want to be happy, smile, and laugh, but this typically starts with what comes out of our mouths. Speaking words of life, hope, and joy make us smile, brings us joy, and encourages those around us.

We all go through tough times, but God desires that we be joyful and happy in every circumstance of life, both in the good and the bad. The Bible says, in 1 Thessalonians 5:16-18, "always be joyful, never stop praying, always be thankful in every circumstance, for this is God's will for you." God knows and sees the setbacks that the enemy tried to inflict on you, and how he continues to try to cause you to feel down and discouraged. However, He does not want us to let the enemy win, rather He wants us to rise and say, "What the enemy meant for evil, my God will turn to good." [2] What the enemy has stolen from me, the years of pain I had to endure and setbacks I had to go through, God is going to restore to me."

When you go through difficulties, use faith-filled words to get you to a higher place. If you come to a situation that looks difficult, instead of saying, "This is too hard, I don't think I can ever accomplish this," instead say, "I can do all things through Christ who strengthens me" (Philippians 4:13). When you go through times of sickness, start by saying, "No, I am coming out of this sickness, you died for my sickness, Lord, and was bruised for my iniquities (sins) and by your stripes, I am healed" (Isaiah 53:5). Speaking words of faith and hope only strengthens us and gets us closer to the place we want to be.

God wants to give you wonderful things. His plans for you are good, to give you hope and a future.[3] However, this future and your destiny can only come about if your mouth comes into agreement with what you want to see. You see, your life is directed by your tongue, which is a small part of our body but has great power. Just like a ship, "although it is very large and is driven by strong winds, this ship is steered by a very small rudder and goes wherever the pilot wants it to go" (James 3:3-4). In the same way, when a bit is placed in a horse's mouth, it can be used to turn the horse's body in a whole different direction.[4] Your tongue can cause your life to move in the direction that you want it to go. That is why it is so important to be careful what you say. Our words can be used as a tool to uplift and edify, or they can be a tool to destroy. Even though the tongue is a small thing, if used in the wrong way, it can start a wildfire (James 3:5).

Jamie was now 34 years old and gulped in thinking how she lived down the life that she had in her old hometown in Missouri. She was never brought up in a Christian home; in fact, she came from a home that was broken not only from the inside but the outside as well. Her father was an alcoholic and her mother was there "but not there," and Jamie felt alone most days. She was hurting on the inside and felt she just needed someone to love her. She ended up getting into a relationship with a boy named John and she felt like for the first time, she was loved. This was her friend, a person that she could see herself with for a lifetime.

Then the rumors started to spread around the school.

Rumors that Jamie was sleeping with John and possibly multiple people began to run rampant throughout the school, and she was called horrible names as a result. As the story was spread from one person to the next it became like a wildfire spreading around the school. Jamie became so overwhelmed by the pain of their words that she thought about committing suicide.

She was turning 18 in one more month and thought to herself, "I have to leave," and eventually she did just that. Many years had passed, and now after becoming a Christian she looked back and thought, "Those kids never really understood how much pain they caused me. Their words were like a dagger in my heart. I was hurting, so depressed, lonely, and had no one to turn to. I needed love, not more pain." After pondering some more she thought, "They will never know how much they hurt me." We can all relate to Jamie's story in one way or another. Have you ever been talked about? Has anyone ever judged you, even though they never really knew your heart or what you were going through? If so, you are not alone.

Our words have the power to either build someone up or tear them down. God says our words should be wholesome (good & beneficial), always full of grace that is considerate and gentle towards everyone. [5] If we cover the offenses and weakness of others, then that same grace will be available for us. However, when a person repeats what they hear and gossips, "it separates the closest of friends" (Proverbs 17:9 ESV). When we come into agreement with God's word and live as He has called us to live, then we will enjoy a life full of happiness, peace, and joy. Galatians 5:22-23 says, "The fruit of the spirit is love, joy, peace, patience, kindness, goodness, faithfulness, gentleness, and self-control."

Those who belong to Jesus Christ have crucified their sinful nature together with its passions and appetites.

Galatians 5:22-23 says, "The fruit of the spirit is love, joy, peace, patience, kindness, goodness, faithfulness, gentleness, and self-control."

This may not always be easy to do; however, we can all strive to be what God has called us to be. He has so many great plans for us, and He is a good God and wants to show us the path that will bring the most blessings to our lives. God wants to fill our mouths with good things, so we can be a blessing to those around us (Psalms 103:5)

Growing up I had a friend in school that I was very close to. When she initially came to our class in the middle of the school year, it was noticeable that she was very thin and smaller in size compared to the kids around us. I could not quite put my finger on it, but I knew something was not right. When she would walk into class, she seemed nervous and appeared stiff. I think about it now and I can imagine how hard it must have been for her. I tried to talk to her, but she would quickly turn toward me, answer questions with a single word and then stare straight ahead at the teacher. She appeared very guarded and tense.

The next few days passed and we were at lunch, and I noticed that she was sitting at lunch by herself. I then went and asked if I could sit next to her. She looked startled and surprised that anyone would want to sit next to her. I started to talk to her. She smiled and was very nice. Over time, she ended up telling me that she had Cystic Fibrosis, which is a life-threatening disease that causes mucus to fill up in her lungs while affecting other organs and eventually causing them to fail. I understood that this was a very sensitive subject for her. Once when we were walking back to class after lunch, some boys walked by and made smart remarks and snickered at her. I gave them a look while she walked quickly with her head down. She was too embarrassed to talk about it. I can only imagine what that must have done to her self-esteem.

Those boys probably did not realize it at the time, but their words had so much power. They had an option to belittle her and make her feel worse, or encourage her and lift her spirits; however, they chose the former. I understood why my friend Emily was so guarded and reserved. When I called her on the phone and we discussed homework, I could hear her struggle to breathe. She told me one day, "Julie, I would really love for you to spend the night at my house, but I have to use an oxygen tank and it's just a lot of equipment that I need, and it's all around me." She did not have to say anymore... I understood.

One year after that, my good friend Emily passed away and I attended her funeral. Her mother was standing at the casket and when she saw me, she asked, "Are you Julie"? I replied yes. She then told me, "I don't think you realize what an impact you made on my daughter's life. She always talked about you, and you were a very special person to her." She stopped and said, "Thank you." My eyes began to fill up with tears, I didn't think that I had done anything special, but it was a friendship that meant a great deal to both of us. Even now, knowing that my friend Emily was impacted, encouraged, and edified before she went to Heaven makes my eyes fill up with tears, and I smile. The truth is you never know who will come across your path, if they are hurting within, or what they are going through. Just a warm smile, a look of acknowledgment, or even a friendly comment may go a long way. You never know the life that can be impacted or the life that you can touch with your words and actions. We ought to choose words that would brighten someone's day, bring them a smile, or encourage them in some way.

God tells us that our tongue has incredible power, and we can use it to bless others and bring life, or curse others and bring death. Often people say that "sticks and stones may break my bones but words will never hurt me," however, we all know this is not true. Our words can be the most difficult thing to control and often we can regret the words we say, especially when we have hurt others. The Bible says, "If you want to enjoy life and see many happy days, keep your tongue from speaking evil and your lips from telling lies" (1 Peter 3:10). You have incredible power to change and impact lives by what you say!

Be Careful What You Say

Miriam loved her brother Moses. However, when he rose to a position of honor and great stature, she started to become envious. She then began to murmur and speak negatively against her brother Moses. Numbers 12 tells us that Miriam and Aaron spoke against Moses because he married an Ethiopian woman, which was different from their Jewish background. Then Miriam said to her brother Aaron, "Has the Lord only spoken through Moses, does He not also speak through us?"

The Bible says that the "Lord heard what they were saying." This is a big deal because it means that not only did God hear their words, but He hears the words that come out of our mouths as well. The Bible describes Moses as a humble, kind, and "the most righteous man on the whole earth." God was angry that Miriam slandered (gossiped and spoke negatively about) her brother because the Lord had chosen him for a specific purpose and plan (see Numbers 12).

We often do not realize that God hears and sees everything we do and say. This is a pretty big deal that lets us know we ought to be careful with what comes out of our mouths. The Lord then called all three, Miriam, Moses, and Aaron, to come out from their tents, and He appeared in a pillar of cloud before them. The Lord said, "I want you to hear what I have to say. If there was a prophet among you, I would have spoken to him in visions and dreams. However, "Moses is the meekest [humble, gentle, and submissive] person on the earth." [1]

Moses was picked amongst the Jews because of his heart. God goes on to say, "So why is it that you are not afraid to speak against *My servant* Moses?" God became angry with Miriam and struck her with leprosy. Aaron and Moses then begged God to heal her and Aaron also asked God for the forgiveness of his own "foolish words." After seven days of confinement, Miriam came out of the camp and Moses cried and prayed to God on her behalf, and only then was she healed of leprosy. [1] We can see here that God was not happy with the words she spoke against her brother Moses, but Miriam, along with her brother Aaron, ended up asking God for forgiveness and mercy, and God forgave them.

> *Your words matter and can make a difference in someone's life.*

The Bible tells us that "what comes out of the mouth proceeds from the heart, and this defiles a man" (Matthew 15:11). God wants good things for us, that is why He instructs us to stay away from doing things that can open the door for the enemy to work in our lives. When we choose to gossip, slander, or hurt people with our words we give the enemy an upper hand, by allowing division among friends, family, and others that we love. The Bible says, "for out of the heart come evil thoughts, murder, adultery, sexual immorality, theft, false witness, and slander. These are things that can ruin and defile a person" (Matthew 5:18-20).

To be careful with our words just means we are to be mindful of what we say and to think before we speak. When we decide to take a moment and think before we speak, we are taking time to honor God's word and obey Him, and obedience will always bring rewards and blessings. I have had my share of trouble in this area. In my younger years, I was very quick to tell people how I felt and was very frank. Over the years I have learned to keep a guard over my mouth and be mindful of what I choose to say. I am sure we have all been in this place, but God does not ask us to do things alone. He has offered His helping hand and His grace to get us through each day. Without His help it would be impossible to do all that He asks us to do.

Jesus is the vine and we are the branches, apart from Him we can do nothing. [2] You and I can use our words to encourage others, lift them with our words and put a smile on their faces. The next time you see your spouse and you want to give him or her a piece of your mind, pause and think, "If I say these words, will I cause us to become more united or divided?" The enemy would love for you to make his job a little bit easier. That is why it is so important to tame our tongue. Our tongue can either make or break our marriage or any other relationship that is important to us. We ought to be mindful of what comes out of our mouths, because words cannot be taken back.

1 Peter 3:10 (AMP) says, "Whoever would love life and see good days must keep their tongue from evil and their lips from deceitful speech." However, taking time to think before you speak, works for your benefit and causes people to actually respect you and listen to what you have to say. [3] This is what God advises us to do in His word. God wants the best for our lives and He gives us His word to show us how to get there. Many people do not want to take the time to control their tongue and pause before speaking; however, the word of God says we will eat the fruit of what we sow (Proverbs 18:21). When you sow seeds of anger and volatile speech, you will get the same results in return. If you sow seeds of love and kindness with your words, you are more likely to bear good fruit.

> 1 Peter 3:10 (AMP) says, "Whoever would love life and see good days must keep their tongue from evil and their lips from deceitful speech."

Life and death are in the power of your tongue[4] and our words, good or bad, affect the ones around us. Have you ever been at work and encountered an employee who always complains and never looks at the bright side of things? You may think in your mind, "I wish she would just be quiet." Or, "She's always complaining and talking about how bad things are in her own life and at work, even though we all do the same job." We have all experienced this at some point or another, but some people always seem to focus only on the negative aspects of their lives rather than focusing on what's good. They talk about how bad things are, what did not go right, and everything wrong. For those of us listening to this, it can cause us to feel more annoyed or irritated, and allows for a negative atmosphere to develop in our area of work, or even in our own lives. No one enjoys being around someone who is always focused on what did not go right, because this causes us to feel sad, darkens our day, and discourages those of us who are listening.

No, if you have an opportunity to speak, use your words to uplift and encourage someone. Bring a little sunshine into the lives of those around you and brighten up the day with your words. If you don't feel happy, spend some time in God's presence where you can get recharged. If you have been feeling sad, mad, or depressed in any way, put everything aside that can distract you, and spend time talking, crying, and sharing your heart with God. He understands. He is ready and waiting with His arms open wide for you, and wants to spend time talking with you.

> *I encourage you to speak words that bring life, love, hope, and healing to those around you.*

After you do this, you will start to notice that you feel lighter, freer, and have a bounce to your step. Jesus wants this for you and His arms are open wide to receive you as you come to Him. He wants to talk with you, share His heart with you, and spend time with you. God wants us to have the best life now and tells us how we can do this through His word. Our words have incredible power to change the lives and the atmosphere of those around us. The next time you choose to speak, I encourage you to speak words that bring life, love, hope, and healing to those around you. When you do this, your heart will begin to rejoice, and the love and power of God will be seen in all that you say and do! You will then be a light that stands on a hill that cannot be hidden, a bright white light for all the world to see! [5]

CHAPTER 2

Your Words Are like Seeds

Our words are like seeds, and eventually they will produce a harvest. The Bible says "that you will reap what you sow (Galatians 6:7). This means that if we speak words, whether positive or negative, we will eventually give birth to what we have been saying or doing over time. We can speak words of love or words of hatred, words of sickness or words of healing, words of staying in debt or becoming debt-free.

What we say matters. Instead of speaking words of "not having enough" speak words of prosperity by saying, "One day I am going to be debt-free, one day I will have victory." It is also important to take the corresponding action that is needed to accomplish what we want to see and what we have been praying for. The corresponding action is needed to bring your results, similar to when you sow a seed. When you sow a seed, you are doing an action that will bring about a harvest. In the same way, when you need a job you will need corresponding action to reap. When you sow a seed of faith you are bound to get results. With faith, nothing is impossible for those that believe (Hebrews 11:6).

With our human senses, we are not able to tell if a seed is alive or not because it is something we cannot see. When you plant a seed in the dirt you are not able to see, feel, hear, smell, or taste it, but we know from experience that one day the seed is going to produce a harvest and we will eat the fruit of our lips (Proverbs 18:21). Every day you are planting seeds in someone around you, whether it is positive or negative seeds. This can also be something we can do to ourselves as well, without even being aware of it.

When I was in high school, math was a very difficult subject for me to understand and grasp. When going through my math homework, I would often say, "This is so hard, I'm not good at math, I hate it and I just can't do it." My mind was made up. I gave in to how I felt rather than saying, "I can do all things through Christ who strengthens me," and I should have actually worked towards getting better. Rather, I spoke just the opposite and it increased my anxiety and fear so that I would automatically cry with thoughts of failure while attempting to work on my math problems.

> *I can do all things through Christ who strengthens me"* (Philippians 4:13).

Then one day a good friend of mine said, "Julie, cry when someone dies, or cry when you are sick, but don't cry about math." When he said these words, it was like a light bulb went off, "I had worked myself into a fit and I started to believe what I was saying, which only made the problem worse." With my friend's words, I wiped my tears, took a deep breath, and "like a big girl" I started to change my thinking and my words. Nothing had changed in my ability to do the math; however, the next time I came across a problem, I would take a deep breath and say, "I can do this, with God's help I can do all things through Christ who strengthens me" (Philippians 4:13). I just began to take a step, another baby step, then one step at a time I was able to work towards getting better and better. I kept my mind open, tamed my emotions and words, and was able to get through, pass the test and the class, and accomplish what I needed to do.

You can do the very same thing. Instead of saying what you cannot do, turn it around and start speaking what you want to see yourself do. You may want to start a business that you have been dreaming about. Start by speaking in the direction that you are seeking and then start making a plan to get there. Or perhaps you want to lose some weight and get healthier. Take one step at a time. For example, you can even say, "Today I am going to walk around the block for two minutes." You may say, "Well, Julie, I'm not going to lose weight by walking for two minutes." However, you are two minutes closer to your goal than you were before. You may start with two minutes and end up doing 15 minutes, or you may stick with 2 minutes, but that is better than doing nothing at all and is one step closer to your goal.

God wants the best for you, and He is your biggest supporter and is cheering you on. It is God's highest wish that "you would prosper and be in good health even as your soul prospers, and that we would glorify him through our bodies" (3 John 1: 2; 1 Corinthians 10:31). Put your vision in front of you, speak your desires daily, and take a step of faith (Habakkuk 2:2). With God's help, nothing will be impossible for you!

Can You Believe and Receive It?

Faith comes from within, and each of us is given a measure of faith that is available for every believer. It is now our job to build that faith by reading God's word, studying scripture, and increasing our knowledge of Him (Romans 12:3, Romans 10:17). For example, we all have muscles, but if we want those muscles to grow then we need to get to the gym and start the process of building ourselves up. This is something that you and I can do if we want to see the wonderful things that God has in store for us.

It is impossible to speak words of defeat and expect victory. Or say, "Oh I will never get well," and expect healing. You must speak in faith about what you want to see happen and walk towards the promise, the dream, or the destiny that God has put in your heart. God has good things in store for you and He wants to give you His very best. However, we must have the "faith to receive what He wants to give us," otherwise we may miss out on wonderful opportunities that lie ahead (Hebrews 11:6).

This is what happened to the Israelites when they attempted to enter the land of Canaan. God wanted to give the Israelites the promised and most prosperous land. He told the Israelites with His own words that it was a good land, flowing with milk and honey, and He would give the Israelites possession over it. Moses then sent out 12 spies and told them to explore and search the land. He said,

"Go up through the Negev and enter the hill country. See what the land is like and whether the people who live there are strong or weak, few or many. What kind of land do they live in? Is it good or bad? What kind of towns do they live in? How is the soil? Is it fertile or poor? Do your best to bring back some of the fruit of the land, because this is the season for fresh ripe grapes"
(See Numbers 13: 17-20 NIV).

The 12 spies that Moses sent out began to scour the land for forty days in search of what they could find and what they could see. After forty days the spies brought a report to Moses and the people of Israel saying, *"We went into the land to which you sent us, and it does flow with milk and honey! Here is its fruit* (Numbers 13:27-28). *But the people who live there are powerful, and the cities are fortified and very large. We even saw descendants of Anak there along with all of their other surrounding enemies"* (see Hebrews 13:27-29). What were these spies saying? In essence, they were saying that "this is too big for us to handle, it is a beautiful place, but there is no way we can defeat those giants. It is impossible for us because we are like "grasshoppers" compared to them." The spies saw themselves as less than and incapable of doing what God told them they could do. Instead, they spoke words of discouragement and defeat rather than speaking words of faith and victory.

I can only imagine the Israelites beginning to panic as fear and anxiety overtook them. Can you imagine the possible thought of going to a land and taking possession of it when the odds seem against you and it seems impossible? However, Caleb (who was also a spy) stepped in and with faith said to Moses and the Israelites, "Let us go up at once and take possession of it; for we will certainly conquer it! "(Numbers 13:30 AMP). Caleb was ready! He believed God's words, had faith, and was ready for action. He had an "I can do it" mindset and his words matched it! But unfortunately, the men who had also gone up to see the land said, "We are not able to go up against the people of Canaan, for they are too big, too strong, and will devour us, for we are like grasshoppers in our sight, and so we are in their sight" (Hebrews 13: 32-33).

Wow, here we have a prime example of what *not* to do. They repeatedly spoke words of doubt, defeat, and discouragement, and gave the Israelites a bad report about the land which they had spied out. Instead of coming into agreement with what God said they could do, the spies said quite the opposite. The Israelites had

> *Your words along with an "I can do it" mindset will cause you to rise higher.*

a perfect opportunity that was right in front of them to conquer a land that was already given by God and would be a blessing to them and their families. However, they did not believe nor had faith, which limited God's ability to bless them. You see, God wants to give us the best of the land, the best of life, but it's up to us to take hold of the promise, because He will not force us to do anything we don't want to or are not willing to do. I often think about what the Israelites said at the end of that text. They said, "We were like grasshoppers in our sight and so we were."

My sister used to say this phrase that changed my life when I was young. One day she said, "Julie, if you think you will not be able to do it, then you won't, but if you think you can do something, then you will." Unfortunately, the Israelites' thoughts and words held them back from

accomplishing all that God had in store for them. This can be true for all of us, but it does not have to be. God has amazing things in store for all of us. Take hold of all that He wants to give to you, because after all, you are a child of the most high God!

Don't Dig up Your Seed

When we plant a seed in the ground, we expect a harvest. We all have desires of maybe wanting to lose 15 lbs., pay off our debt, or get healed. Often, many of us start by getting excited, digging the dirt up, holding our precious seed of faith in the light, and planting it while praying for a miracle. We start with faith, and most of us often start charged by saying, "This year I'm going to pay all those credit cards off. " Or, "I am going to lose 10 pounds this month." However, when our goals start to get a bit more difficult, we get tempted to say, "There's no way I'll ever pay this off," or "I can't lose those 15 pounds. It's just too hard." It is easy for us to give up with our attitudes, actions, and words, and dig up the seeds that we sowed because we do not see results right away. Instead, when we plant our seed of faith, we ought to press into God and keep that desired seed underground, watering it with our continued prayers and shining the sun of God's word over it daily. The sunshine of the word of God is what keeps that plant energized and living. When we declare the rays of God's written word and promises over our desired seed, then we know it will sprout up in due time if we do not give up or dig it up with words of doubt and unbelief.

The Bible says, "that death and life are in the power of the tongue (Proverbs 18:21) and eventually we will eat its fruit." It can indeed be difficult when we don't see results right away; however, if we don't give up, we will eventually see the harvest of our prayers. Galatians 6:9 says, "Let us not grow weary or become discouraged in doing good, for at the proper time we will reap if we do not give up!" When we live in faith, we please God with our faith, so don't give up but keep pressing forward. Grab ahold of God's word, declare His blessing and promises over and over again in your life. When you do this, the word of God becomes rooted in your spirit and nothing will be able to shake your faith and you will receive the fruit of your seed.

> *"That death and life are in the power of the tongue (Proverbs 18:21) and eventually we will eat its fruit."*

There was a drought in Israel because of King Ahab's disobedience to God. King Ahab was considered a wicked king amongst all the other kings that had reigned before him. He had disobeyed and dishonored God by creating an altar and worshiping the idol Baal. He led the nation of Israel into worshiping the idol Baal as well, which angered God. As a result of his disobedience, God caused a drought to come upon Israel for 3 years (see 1 Kings 16). The drought was very difficult to bear, but after the nation of Israel realized that the God of Israel was the one true God, they cried out for forgiveness. Elijah then told Ahab, "Go and eat for I hear an abundance of rain coming!" Elijah prophesied the answer to the problem even before he saw the results! He used his words to declare victory even before he saw the answer.

Elijah believed God was able to do anything on his behalf, so he started to pray. The Bible says, "He put his head in between his knees and began to pray." This is interesting to me, and I think to myself, "Why did he need to do this?

Why not just sit or stand up praying?" I believe Elijah did this to stay focused and remain completely in tune with receiving an answer from the Lord. You see, he planted a seed of faith for rain, then he began to shower it with his continual faith and persistent prayer until he saw the answer. Elijah prayed and asked his servant to continue to look out towards the sea for the answer. He prayed with expectation and continued to watch and wait for God to move on his behalf.

Elijah continued to pray and ask his servant to continue looking once, twice, three and even six times. However, there remained no answer to his requests. Elijah could have easily given up, become frustrated, and said, "Forget it, there is no use in praying, it does not look like God is going to answer." However, he knew that if he persisted God would open the door and answer his prayers.[1]

Matthew 7:7 says, "Keep on asking, and you will receive what you ask for. Keep on seeking, and you will find. Keep on knocking, and the door will be opened for you." God wants us to keep believing until we receive the answer as His word says. This is exactly what Elijah did, with his head between his knees and focused on God's spirit. He again began to pray and asked his servant to look for the answer. On the seventh time, the servant yelled and said, "I saw a cloud, I saw a little cloud, it's the size of a man's hand rising from the sea! (1 Kings 18:44).

Even though the prayer took some time to be answered, Elijah finally received the answer to his prayer. Though there was only a little cloud of hope that arose, Elijah yelled to his servant in excitement and said, "Go tell Ahab to get in his chariot and go home, if not, the rain will stop him!" [2] The cloud that looked so small and insignificant began to grow and grew into a mighty rainstorm. In the same way, often the answer to our prayers may come slowly, or appear insignificant at first, but do not dig up your seed of faith. Instead, stay focused with your eyes on God, expect your answer, and persist in prayer until you receive what you are praying for. God is pleased when we pray in faith and are believing Him for the answer. The Bible says, "The effectual and fervent prayer of a righteous man (is powerful and effective) and availeth much" (James 5:16).

> *God wants good things for your life*

The more time you spend in prayer, seeking and obeying God, the more confident you will feel that your heart's desires match his will for you. The Father wants us to have good things and wants us to remain in faith, persist in prayer, and keep on asking until we receive the answer to our prayers. Often when we plant a seed, which is our prayer request, along with faith, we can dig up that seed by saying things like, "I'm not sure if this is going to happen," "This seems impossible," or, "This is too hard."

When we speak words of defeat, we cannot expect victory. In the same way, if you dig up your seeds with negativity, doubt, and unbelief you cannot expect the answer to your prayers. [3] God wants to give you the desires of your heart,[4] He loves you so much. Continue to trust Him with your life, walk in His ways, and remember, don't dig up your seed of faith for the thing that you are believing for, no matter how impossible it seems!

CHAPTER 3

Changing Directions

Did you know that words can change the direction that your life goes in? Some people don't even realize this is possible, but it's true. The words you say can impact your attitude and then your actions. These actions can then determine where your life is headed and ultimately impact your future. Just think of your profession, as an example. You may never have been a preacher, lawyer, nurse, journalist, business owner, or the position you are in now if your words were going against what you were trying to achieve.

In other words, you need to speak in the direction that you seek. Instead of listing all the negative reasons why you cannot do something, list all the positive reasons why you can accomplish the task that you desire to complete. For example, if you desire to build a house but the words coming out of your mouth are opposite to what you want to achieve, you may not be able to get to your destination.

Making statements like, "I don't think I can come out of debt," "I don't think I can pass that class," or, "This seems impossible" will not help you get any closer to reaching your goal.

Rather than speaking words of doubt and disbelief, start speaking what you seek and list all the reasons why you *can* accomplish and reach your goals. Whether we realize it or not, negative continual words will become our reality. The Bible says, "so shall my word be that goes out from my mouth; it will not come back to me empty, but it will accomplish what I purposed and shall succeed in the thing for which I sent it" (Isaiah 55:11). Our word will not come back to us unfulfilled; it will accomplish everything we sent it to accomplish. Are the words that you speak about your life pushing you toward your purpose and destiny, or pulling you away from it?

Jennifer was a young woman who worked as a secretary in an executive office. She would often talk to her best friend Kate about how she dreamed of being a nurse. Kate tried her best to encourage her friend to accomplish her dreams, even if she had to do it little by little. Jennifer was living in a two-and-a-half-bedroom apartment with her friend and listed all the reasons why she would not be able to become a nurse. She said, "Oh, I just don't have the money, my rent is too high and it's just been so long since I have been in school."

However, the truth is that this dream remained very important to her because she would continue to talk about it often. Kate then tried to create a plan for her. "Why don't you downsize and get a one-bedroom apartment, take out a small loan, and take it one step at a time? Also, I found out that once you get to the hospital and become a nurse, they have a program that will help you repay all your loans." Kate was excited about the possibilities! However, this did not persuade Jennifer, because she had already created a negative mindset by saying, "I don't think it's possible, it's not doable, and I would have to make sacrifices." Unfortunately, Jennifer did not understand that she would only need to make small sacrifices that would cause *short-term pain for long-term gain.*

She could not see that if she were to downsize to a one-bedroom apartment, take out a small loan, get focused, and find ways to move forward, that eventually, she would get to a place of financial stability. She then could move out of her apartment to buy a larger house and be able to come out of debt and accomplish her dreams. However, her limited mindset and continual negative words prevented her from accomplishing all that God had in store for her. The good news is that we don't have to live like this! God wants to give us good things, and He is the one that gives us the desires

> *God wants to give us good things*

of our hearts, but we have the responsibility of using our words, resources, and doing our best to get where we need to be while we trust in Him.

The words of our mouth have control over our lives, whether we admit it or not. What comes out of your mouth will determine your future. The words you speak can even influence the way you act and feel, as well as determine the attitude and outlook on your life. No matter what it is we are attempting to communicate, getting our point across starts with choosing our words wisely. The Bible says, "When you put bits into a horse's mouth you can guide and control his whole body." In the same way, "as a rudder controls the direction of a ship your tongue can control the direction that your life will go in" (see James 3:3-4). God made man to be an overseer not only over the earth, but over our mouths as well. What you say and your present attitude can impact your tomorrow.

An individual in the Bible whose course was changed by his actions, words, and attitude was Naaman. Naaman was known as a mighty commander in the Syrian Army. He was highly respected by the king for his courage, strength, and the many victories he had won during battle. However, amid his prestige, he struggled with a condition called leprosy, which I could imagine was very embarrassing for a man of such valor. Naaman's wife had a servant girl that felt sorry for him and knew that he could only get healed through a miracle. She suggested that Naaman go and see a prophet in Samaria named Elisha that could heal him of leprosy.

Naaman rounded up his horses, and standing tall, was ready to meet Elisha and receive his healing. When his servant knocked on the door, Elisha did not come out and instead sent a messenger to tell him to go wash in the Jordan river seven times for his healing. Naaman was furious. He said, "I thought he would at least come out and see me, call on his God and heal me." [1] However, Elisha did not do this and Naaman was furious. He then said, "Don't we have better rivers in Aram than this dirty Jordan river in Israel?" [2] He reared up his horses to go when his servant begged him to stay and just be obedient to what the man of God was asking him to do. Naaman was getting ready to go home when his servant begged him to be obedient to what

> *Your continual negative words can keep you from God's best*

Elisha had asked him to do. Naaman reluctantly agreed. I can imagine him saying, "I am not going to do this, I am better than this, this is an ugly river anyway."

However, with his servant's requests, he pushed his pride aside, became obedient, and got his healing. It is scary to think that his words of doubt and negativity could have caused him to miss out on the very miracle he desperately needed. Do you speak words of doubt and disbelief over your situation? God wants you to have everything that you need; however, your negative words can keep you from obtaining the very wonderful thing that God wants to give you. If you struggle in this area, pray and ask God for his help and start speaking words of hope, faith, and victory. You will be so glad that you did!

Where the Mind Goes the Mouth Follows

Where the mind goes, the mouth follows. This is such a true statement and is just a part of human nature. Our minds are powerful and

> "As someone thinks within himself, so he is" (Proverbs 23:7).

will shape who we are and what we will become. The Bible says, "As someone thinks within himself, so he is" (Proverbs 23:7). What you think about yourself matters, and is directly tied into your words. Whatever you decide that you are, is what you will be. If you say, "I don't think I will ever get that job," then you have already decided in advance that you will not be getting the job that you desired. Instead, think about all the reasons why you should get the job, start making a list, and repeat it to yourself so that your repeated words will build faith and the confidence you need to move forward.

There was a time in my life when I had never learned this truth. Whatever thought came into my mind I accepted. I would never question the source of the thought, but rather just believed it. One day, I was crying to my sister about how inadequate I felt in achieving a goal and not being able to do well in a school subject. She then abruptly said, "If you say you are not able to do it, then you can't, but if you say that you can, then you will be able to!" You are who you say you are.

This was a light bulb moment for me, and I was shocked she said this! I started to think about the statement my sister said, and I realized that my words had power. I then made a conscious decision not to put myself down in my thoughts or words and determined that this was the start of a new direction in my life. The Bible says in Philippians 4:8, "Finally, brothers, think on whatever is true, whatever is honorable, whatever is just, whatever is pure, whatever is lovely, whatever is commendable, if there is any excellence, if there is anything worthy of praise, think about these things." If we live a life according to God's will, and follow His ways and do what the Bible says, then we will reap the rewards of His promise.

Elijah was a prophet that God used in mighty ways. He performed many miracles, was a prayer warrior, and able to do the extraordinary through God's power. God had used Elijah to destroy the prophets of Baal and he was used mightily for the Lord's work. When King Ahab informed Queen Jezebel that Elijah's God had destroyed her prophets of Baal, she declared that she would kill Elijah as well (1 Kings 19).

When Elijah heard the news, he ran for his life and hid in a cave. He became depressed and allowed negative thoughts to fill his head. He was tired and told God that he had enough and wanted God to take his life. Instead, God met his basic needs and sent an angel to give food and drink and to offer him a time of rest and rejuvenation. After he had rested, he again traveled another 40 days and came to another cave, where he slept once more. Elijah, after doing great miracles and showing others that God was alive and living, now hid in a cave and did not remember the great miracles that he just performed (see I Kings 19).

His mind was being flooded with thoughts of doubt, depression, and discouragement. God then came to Elijah and said,

"What are you doing here Elijah?" Elijah complained and said, "I have zealously served the LORD God Almighty. But the people of Israel have broken their covenant with you, torn down your altars, and killed every one of your prophets. I am the only one left, and now they are trying to kill me, too." (1 Kings 19:14)

God then showed Elijah through a powerful wind that broke the mountain into pieces, an earthquake, fire, and a whisper that he was God and able to do all things. God told Elijah that the wicked house of Ahab would be rooted out, the people of Israel would be punished for their sins, and let him know that he was not the only man of God standing.

You see, Elijah thought he was the only prophet alive and let his mind race off into a direction that was farthest from the truth. God corrected Elijah and said,

Our thoughts can impact our words and ultimately our destiny

29

"You are not the only prophet left." Rather, he had 7,000 other prophets that had never bowed down to Baal (1 Kings 19:17). Nevertheless, Elijah continued to repeat the same negative thoughts to God once more. This time God decided to replace Elijah with a man named Elisha who would do greater miracles than he.

Unfortunately, Elijah's thoughts impacted his attitude and ultimately his words. He told God that he was not able to complete the task that God had before him, and so God used someone else instead. Our thoughts can affect the words that come from our mouths and can ultimately affect our destiny. If you want to reach your highest potential in life, make sure you say what God says about you and not what the enemy wants you to believe. You are a child of the most high King, and He desires that you and I think on the things that are above and not focus on thoughts that are contrary to His word (Colossians 3:2).

CHAPTER 4

Environmental Hazards

Our environment has the power to affect our minds, which then can affect our words. Often when we think of the environment, we think more along the lines of nature and the earth that surrounds us. However, it is our environment that impacts our lives. Our environment includes the people we associate with, our friends, family, loved ones, or anyone that we come into a relationship with. Our environment also includes the things we see, hear, and smell along with the words that we use each day consistently.

Many people are a product of their environments. The environment surrounding you can affect your behaviors, attitudes, and the words with which you communicate. Often, if you have come from a home that was chaotic or crazy versus calm and controlled, you tend to exhibit those same characteristics because this is what is common and familiar to you. However, if you find that your environment does not benefit you, then it's time to make a change. The good news is that God is willing and able to help you do this.

Changes in our environment and our lives are possible if you do things one step at a time. You may not know where to start, or how to begin changing your environment, but everything in life begins with a step. If you are not happy with your environment, make a conscious decision today to do something about it. God wants the best for you and he will take you by the hand and guide you if you are willing. Let Him do the work that He wants to do in you and be open to His guidance, which has been outlined in the word of God.

Who Do You Associate With?

1 Corinthians 15:33 "Do not be misled: 'Bad company corrupts good character.'"

The Bible teaches us that who we associate with or call our friends can impact our behaviors and our thought processes. Our marriages, friendship, and relationships with others can indirectly influence the direction of our lives. That is why who we are in relationships with is very important. The Bible says in Proverbs 22:24-25, "Do not make friends with people who have poor character (hot-tempered, angry, or unwise) or you may learn their ways and get yourself ensnared." This can be applied to any behavior that our friends may have. Who we associate with influences our lives and our character, actions, and speech whether we realize it or not.

Proverbs 13:20, "Walk with the wise and become wise, walk with fools and you will suffer harm."

Have you ever noticed that if you hang out with critical and judgmental people, you also tend to be judgmental and critical as well? Or if you choose to hang out with people of wisdom, you often tend to act or function in the way they do? God says in Proverbs 13:20, "Walk with the wise and become wise, walk with fools and you will suffer harm." This verse is pretty self-explanatory: if you want to be wise you should hang out with those who are wise; however, if you want to hang out with those who are considered fools, then you will most likely end up just like them. That is why it is important to surround yourself with people that will pull you up rather than down. The Bible says, "Do not be deceived: 'Bad company ruins good morals'" (1Corinthians 15:33).

We often become more like those that we associate with because our spirits are transferable and we act similar to the behaviors that surround us. The choices, lifestyles, and behaviors of those around us can influence our lives and eventually affect our character. If you are surrounded by a negative person all day long, their negative spirit actions and words can get into your heart and soon can create unwanted changes (see Proverbs 22:24-25). Stay away from people that you do not want to be like. The enemy loves to influence our minds and thoughts in any way he can. When we make the choice to surround ourselves with people that do not share the same morals or convictions, we open the door for Satan to come into our hearts and do the damage he so desperately wants to do and change our character. These next few tips are ways in which we can protect ourselves from falling into Satan's traps.

Don't Ignore the Red Flags

If your life is not going in the direction you have wanted or desired it may be best to evaluate your surroundings and be honest with yourself. Is the environment or the people that surround you headed in the direction you are hoping to go in? If not, it is time to make a change. Surrounding yourself with negative people, bad influences, or people who bring you down will inhibit your growth and future potential.

If you find yourself saying, "I am going to spend some time with these friends, but I know my limits and I'm not going to do what they do, or say what they say," this is a red flag that can cause you to stumble and go in the wrong direction. It is often easy to think that we will not fall. 1 Corinthians 10:12-13 (AMP) says, "Therefore let the one who thinks he stands firm [immune to temptation, being overconfident and self-righteous], take care that he does not fall [into sin and condemnation]." Temptation does not come our way with bright flashing lights, saying, "Here I come, I'm going to destroy your life." Rather, the enemy comes in such a sneaky and skillful way that you will not even realize it. Before you know it, you may be going in a direction that you never intended. It is so important not to justify being around people that are not good for us. The Bible says that "the enemy is like a roaring lion, waiting to devour us at our weakest moments" (1 Peter 5:8). Therefore, we ought to "be careful and give no place to the devil" (Ephesians 4:27).

Keep Your Guardrails Up

1. Keep your Guardrails up: if you find yourself becoming someone you are not. If you feel this way, take a moment to evaluate your life and pinpoint the area when the problem began. Through subtle and indirect ways people's lives can influence your behavior. If you find your family or loved ones

saying, "You have changed," and it's not a change that personally brings you peace, then it's time to make a change that will keep you in right standing with God first, and those that love and have your best interest at heart. When our personality and behavior changes, so do our words.

2. Put your Guardrails up: if you find yourself compromising your convictions and are feeling pressured to conform to others. If this is happening, it's time to declare a "time out" and put a stop to those in your life that may be pulling you down. To be honest, why be around a group of friends that do not respect you for being you, and try to downplay your convictions? The truth is that these types of relationships are not good for you and only take you in a direction you do not want to go in.

3. Lastly, put your Guardrails up: if you find yourself being dishonest about an action that you may know in your spirit is wrong or could pull you down. If this happens to you, this is a total red-flag and something the enemy is just waiting for you to be a part of. 1 Peter 5:8 ESV says, "Be sober-minded, be watchful, your adversary the devil prowls around like a roaring lion, seeking someone to devour."

Our relationships and surroundings can influence our behaviors, actions, and words. Surround yourself with people that are good for you and have your best interest at heart. These are people that want to see you live a victorious life and want the best for you. If you find something or someone in your social life that is pulling you down, then you need to make a change so that they will not keep you from all that God has in store for you. The Bible says it best, "Do not be misled: 'Bad company corrupts good character'" (1 Corinthians 15:33, NIV). Make sure the people around you only cause you to move closer to God, not further away, and ask God to guide and direct your steps as your trust in Him each day.

Learning the Hard Way

Samson was a man that God had set apart, who was gifted with the ability to have supernatural strength to do God's work. God wanted to use Samson to accomplish His purpose by rescuing the Israelites from the Philistine's hands. God told Samson's mother not to drink wine nor cut his hair, and to obey all the commands He was giving her. Samson's mom was now aware that his strength lay in his hair. As Sampson grew into adulthood, he became more prideful of his natural abilities. He then began to have an eye for beautiful women and his lusts began to grow. Despite the advice of his parents and the social customs to marry a woman from his own heritage, Samson saw a beautiful Philistine woman and desired her. His God-intended purpose was to deliver the Israelites from the hand of the Philistines; rather, he loved a woman from that very same background.

His parents advised him and said, "Is there no woman among the daughters of your relatives, or all our people, that you must go to take a wife from the uncircumcised (pagan) Philistines?" However, Samson did not listen and asked them to get Delilah for him, as his body longed for hers. Samson had made several mistakes with women by choosing the wrong ones - despite the advice of his parents. Then ended up meeting his girlfriend Delilah

(Judges 16). Once again, the Philistines were utilizing their very own people such as Delilah to accomplish their mission.

The Philistines asked Delilah to find the secret of what made Samson so strong. They bribed her with money, and she was very interested in the offer. She groaned, moaned, cried, and used her manipulative tactics to get Samson to tell her his secret. Eventually, Samson gave in and told her everything despite the multiple times that she tried to deceive him. I am not sure if Samson was completely blinded, or just loved her so much that he did not care. However, eventually, she caused him to lose his God-given strength and made him captive to the Philistines.

Samson associated with a woman that was no good for him. God's words to Samson were to obey his parent's words of advice to receive his full blessings. Yet despite all of Samson's mistakes and failures, God still had mercy on him, loved him, and gave him justice. In the end, Samson was able to destroy the Philistines with God's help and gained the victory. In the same way, God may often place godly men and women in our lives to help direct us on the right path, and in this case, he used Samson's parents to help guide his way.

> "Therefore if anyone hears these words of mine and puts them into practice, he is like a wise man who builds his house on the rock" (Matthew 7:24).

Samson's parents were older in years and they walked upright before the Lord. The Lord specifically placed them as an overseer of Samson to help guide him in the way he should go; however, he was not open to their words of advice nor counsel. [1] Psalms 37:30 says the mouths of the righteous utter wisdom, and their tongues speak what is just. Samson, unfortunately, became wise in his own eyes and felt that he did not need to heed the warnings of his parents. [2] It is often easy to disregard the counsel of those around us; however, a wise person takes time to stop and listen.[3] We can estimate that Samson's life most likely would have been different if he would have had an open ear, or even inquired of the Lord before he decided to move forward; however, this was not the case. God wants the best for us and that is why He has given us His word to help instruct us in the way that we should go. The Bible is not just a mere book that we should read and take lightly, but it is alive, powerful, and active, and can change your whole life and your future. God says, "Therefore if anyone hears these words of mine and puts them into practice, he is like a wise man who builds his house on the rock" (Matthew 7:24). For even if the wind blows and the oceans surge your foundation will remain strong and you will always remain standing, no matter what!

Conversations

"Do not let unwholesome [foul, profane, worthless, vulgar] words ever come out of your mouth, but only such speech as is good for building up others, according to the need and the occasion, so that it will be a blessing to those who hear [you speak]."
(Ephesians 4:29 AMP)

We have conversations every day. We converse with family, friends, people at work, and pretty much everyone that we come into contact with. Conversations, and what we often talk about, is something that we do every day.

Often, we are surrounded by good conversations, and then there are some bad conversations that do not edify or build us up in any way. However, the Bible advises us to stay away from people that have an unwholesome talk. The word "unwholesome" refers to words that are damaging, harmful, destructive, or causing someone to feel hurt. Instead, our words should be good, something that edifies people and builds them up, offering love and grace to those who hear it (Proverbs 15:1 NIV).

I think this verse is an eye-opener and something many of us have probably struggled with. It is very common as humans to criticize, compare, and look down on people who are not just like us. Often when we see people that live contrary to our lifestyles, we judge and criticize them. During the beginning days of my Christian walk, I did the very same thing. However, through life experiences and understanding the word of God more fully, I came to realize that "not judging someone" is

> *Judge not and you will not be judged*
> *(Matthew 7:1)*

not something God meant for someone else to do, but something He wanted *me* to do. I remember reading the Bible one day and I came upon the verse "do not judge others, or you will be judged" (Matthew 7:1-6). For some reason, that verse was blaring in my face, like it never did before.

I read this verse and knew God was speaking to me. I tried to make changes in my life and now feel that I have come a long way from where I used to be. My family, along with multiple people around the world, have learned these lessons through life experiences and have come to realize this for themselves. God is asking that we avoid speech, conversations, or words that do not build someone up.

Rather He wants us to offer grace to everyone that we come in contact with because we do not know what other people have gone through. We also do not know what their life stories have been and what kind of muddy waters they have had to cross.

Some people make the wrong choices in life because they are looking for love, or maybe there is a void in their life that they are trying to fill. They need someone to show them love instead of pointing the finger at them in condemnation. Instead, the Bible says if we see obvious sin, we are to gently guide people to truth (Galatians 6:1) with the hope that through your gentle spirit God will grant them repentance and lead them into the knowledge of the truth. (2 Timothy 2:25, NIV). We can never *hate* someone to Christ, but we can *love* someone to Christ with our words, love, and actions.

> "Let the one who has never sinned throw the first stone!" (John 8:7).

Jesus Christ was a perfect example of this in John 8 when he was at the temple teaching. The Pharisees and teachers of religious laws brought a woman in front of Jesus that was caught in the middle of adultery. They threw her in front of the crowd to embarrass her and make her feel worthless and ashamed. The Pharisees knew that Jesus would try to help her. They planned to trap the son of God in doing or saying something that they could use against Him. They were downright snakes because they were cunning and malicious in their attempts to discredit Christ. However Jesus, knowing their thoughts and the wicked intent of their heart, began to write in the sand. The Pharisees began to grow impatient and demanded an answer from Him on what they should do with the women. Jesus then said, "Let the one who has never sinned throw the first stone!" (John 8:7). He then began to write in the sand once again.

I have to say I love Jesus for doing this, He was so gracious and humble not to directly accuse the Pharisees with their sin, but indirectly and with a gentle approach He showed the areas that they needed correction in as well. After Jesus rose from the sand a second time, the Pharisees and religious leaders with their stones in hand began to drop them one by one. They knew that they too had sinned in different ways and did not have the right to criticize this adulterous woman of her sins. The oldest from the youngest began to drop their stones one by one, until only the lady and Jesus were left.

He then asked her, with love and kindness in His eyes, "Woman, where are your accusers?" In essence saying, "We all have sinned, not just you, and there is no one left here to condemn you and bring you to shame." Jesus says, "I love you and do not condemn you either, but go and sin no more." Jesus with His words, love, and actions gently instructed her to change her ways and guided her to the truth. I am sure she must have gone home, got on her knees, and thanked God not only for saving her from death but for the mercy and love He had shown to her. Jesus always spoke with words that were kind and compassionate to the hurting and this is the type of attitude and view of others that He wants us to have.

Negative Pictures

Have you ever been with a group of friends who talk about someone in a negative way? Let's say they are talking about a girl named Tina, who you have never met. You have no idea who Tina is, but subconsciously what they have done is painted a negative picture in your mind of their thoughts and experiences with her. Based on their input and remarks, you start to formulate thoughts and impressions of who she is even though you don't even know her. Suddenly, one week later, it just so happens that you end up meeting Tina. She seems to be a nice person, but you cannot seem to get the thoughts of what others have said about her out of your mind.

Has anyone ever painted a negative picture of you that was not true by what they have said about you? Whether it is at work, school,

> *Jesus is gentle and compassionate to those that are hurting*

or in your social setting, this is something that often happens to most of us. People can paint pictures of us by saying things that may not necessarily be true. Someone can slander you by saying that you have done something that may be far from the truth; however, people tend to believe what they hear, rather than what they have seen for themselves.

Joseph felt the same way. He was an innocent man who was lied about and blamed for things he had never done. He was taken to Egypt as a slave, into Potiphar's house. Potiphar was one of Pharaoh's officials and the captain of the guard. He bought Joseph as a slave and allowed him to live in his home. Although Joseph had been through so much heartache, which his brothers had put him through, God was with Joseph in the midst of it and gave him success in everything that he did, which Potiphar recognized. Potiphar trusted Joseph and put him in charge of his entire household and everything he owned because of the favor God had given him.

One day when Joseph was alone, Potiphar's wife came to him and said, "Come to bed with me." Joseph had a nice body and was handsome and she probably could not keep her eyes off of him and lusted after him... However, Joseph was a trustworthy person and feared God. He said to her "Your husband has trusted me with everything he owns, and there is no one second to him that is greater than I. He has given me everything except you because you are his wife. How could I do such a wicked thing? It would be a great sin against your husband and God" (Genesis 39: 8-9). Nonetheless, she kept pressuring Joseph daily, yet he refused to sleep with her. One day when he was alone in a room by himself "she came and grabbed him by his coat and demanded that he sleep with her. He tore himself away but left his coat in her hands as he ran out of the house" (Genesis 39:12).

She was so angry that she began to scream and cry saying, "This Hebrew boy that my husband brought into this house has made a fool of us. He came to rape me, but I screamed and he ran, but left his coat behind." Joseph was innocent and trustworthy, yet Potiphar's wife lied about him and caused all the people that knew him to believe the same. How could this be? He was only trying to do the right thing; however, Potiphar's wife lied about him. She painted a negative picture of who he was and what he had done to the men and women standing around her. Even though these men that had known him for years never saw deceit in him, they believed her lie. Her words impacted his life in enormous ways and he was thrown into prison as a result.

In the same way, our words have the power to either create a negative or positive impression upon others. The Bible says, "Don't use foul, abusive [corrupting or unwholesome] language. Let everything you say be good and helpful so that your words will be an encouragement to those who hear them" (Ephesians 4:29 NLT). We all want others to speak highly of us and say good things about us. It makes us feel happy and brings a smile to our faces. In the same way, we ought to offer grace to others that make mistakes, say or do the wrong thing, or just do not think as we do. We have all been guilty of doing this at some point in our lives, but we can all strive to be more like Jesus and do what He would do.

> God has great plans for you and wants you to receive His best

The next time you want to create a negative picture of others, offer grace as you would want them to do for you. Jesus spoke well of those who hated Him and offered them forgiveness and grace. God has great plans for you and wants you to receive His best. When we come into agreement with His word and follow His advice and instructions, we open the door for God's wonderful blessings and the great things He has in store for us!

Sights, Sounds, and Surroundings

When I was in college I would drive to school, church, and wherever I needed to go with music always playing in the background. Most often I turned the radio dial to my favorite music station, (aka) "The love station." This type of music was slow, mostly romantic, and the lovey-dovey kind that we all come across. One day after listening to this station for months, I started to notice that I was feeling more lonely, sad, and bummed out about not finding a guy or being in a relationship. It got to the point that over time I felt like crying while listening to the music, and became more emotional throughout the day. After a few months of the same saga, I thought to myself, "Why am I feeling like this? Where are all these thoughts coming from?" I then realized it was the music I was listening to, day in and day out. The music I was listening to impacted my life and my emotions in ways that I was not aware of, nor realized.

Studies have shown that music stimulates emotions through specific brain circuits and can easily change the moods we are in. Have you ever noticed that when you put an upbeat song on it makes people smile and begin to dance to the rhythm? In the same way, listening to soft sad music can also bring your mood down as well. Whatever we watch or listen to, and who we decide to surround ourselves with, can impact our lives in various ways. If we listen to negative music, watch violent television shows, or surround ourselves with negative people, this will eventually bring us down emotionally and spiritually, and can affect our behavior, attitude, and words. [1]

Over time we don't even realize our behavior is changing until one day we start to wonder, "Why have I been so sad, mad, or more emotional lately?" It is undeniably a great amount of the things that we feed our soul and spirit with. [2] Psalms 19:14 says, "Let the words of my mouth and meditation of my heart be acceptable in thy sight, oh Lord, my strength and my redeemer." Even though it was a bit hard in the beginning, I consciously decided to change the music to a more uplifting station. I would sing along with the words and realized my mood was being uplifted and I felt more encouraged.

Has this ever happened to you? Have you ever been in a pleasant mood, and then listened to something sad or watched a scary movie for the night, and you notice that your mood begins to shift or change? Most people start to feel a sense of fear, insecurity, or maybe even have nightmares as a direct result of this. Not everything that we see, hear, or are a part of is beneficial for us. 1 Thessalonians 5:22 (AMP) says, "Abstain from evil [shrink from it and keep aloof from it] in whatever form or whatever kind it may be."

There may be times that we may need to say, "Hey, you know what, that movie does not help me in any way, but it just brings me down. I would rather spend my time watching uplifting or encouraging movies or music that does not produce feelings of insecurity, fear, sadness, nor loneliness." Instead, the Bible tells us that we ought to guard our hearts and think on things that are right, pure, true, honorable, lovely, and admirable. We are to think about excellent things, of good report and worthy of praise (Philippians 4:8 NLT).

> *Think on things that are right, pure, true, honorable, lovely and admirable.*
> *(Philippians 4:8 NLT)*

When we feel encouraged and lighthearted, we pass on our feelings and emotions and speak to others based on what we have been feeding our spirit. Our words are directly correlated to who we surround ourselves with and the things which we feed our inner man. God wants us to have an abundant life filled with love and joy and His word teaches us that. Whatever we watch, whatever we listen to, and whoever we associate with can impact our lives subconsciously even if we do not see the results immediately. We all need to keep a guard over our hearts, minds, and mouth which will keep us in victory. I would like to encourage you, the next time you watch or listen to something, to evaluate how it makes you feel. If it is negative or brings you down in any way, be courageous enough to take a stand and decide to make a change in your life for the better. When you do this, you will find that your spirit will be lifted, you will feel light-hearted, and God's joy will fill your heart and mind.

CHAPTER 5

Emotional Impact

Words can cause emotional pain and scarring, or they can lift us up and encourage us to a point that we can feel that we are on the Moon. Positive words bring positive feelings whereas negative words bring negative feelings. It is important to let others know that they are loved, accepted, forgiven, worthy, and a child of the Most High King. As a child of God, we are to offer a kind word to those that are hurting. If we have God in our hearts then our fruits, which include our [actions, attitude, and lifestyle], will show it. *Galatians 5:22-23 says, "But the fruit of the Spirit is love, joy, peace, patience, kindness, goodness, faithfulness, gentleness, and self-control." We ought to let our* conversations always be full of grace, [which are found in the fruits of the spirit] so that we can help those when they need it (Colossians 4:6).

There is a common saying that we often hear that "sticks and stones may break my bones but words will never hurt me." However, this is the farthest from the truth because words do hurt us, but they do not have to have power over us unless we give them power. People may have spoken negative words over you, but don't let their words get inside of you. God sees you as a beautiful shining light. He sees a man or a woman who is worth it all and has so many wonderful qualities and characteristics.

Satan uses the words of others who are not in right standing with God to bring you down. There are supernatural wars that are going on in the spirit realm that we are not aware of that we can read about in the book of Daniel. "For we do not wrestle against flesh and blood [People] but our fight is against the rulers, against the authorities, against cosmic powers over this present darkness, and against the spiritual forces of evil in the heavenly places" (Ephesians 6:12). Satan uses people to try to break you down - but don't let him! He wants to steal your joy, your peace, and all that God has ordained for you. However, God came to give life and the ability to live more abundantly

Growing up I did not realize how important reading God's word was. That is why I cannot stress enough that we ought to find out what God wants to teach us and the things He wants us to do. God's word brings life, peace, and joy; however, we need to be obedient to every word that is written in the Bible. The Bible is our instruction book for life. God's word protects us, guides us, gives us direction, and offers us the best life possible if we are willing to take it. 2 Timothy 3:16-17 says, "All scripture is God-breathed and is useful for teaching, rebuking, correcting, and training in righteousness,

> God's word protects, guides us and gives us direction

so that the servant of God may be thoroughly equipped for every good work." When you put God's word in your heart and fight with the armor of God, you become ready to fight any negative attack that comes your way. Decide to combat the lies of the enemy today and speak only what God says about you in His word.

Guard Your Mouth

"Whoever would love life and see good days must keep their tongue from evil and their lips from deceitful speech." 1 Peter 3:10 (NIV)

The Bible says, "What goes into someone's mouth is not what defiles them, but what comes out of their mouth is what defiles them" (Matthew 15:11). I am sure we have all been in a situation like this before. God is concerned about what comes out of our mouths, and what we have to say. The Bible says, "He hears what we say and one day we will have to give Him an account on the day of judgment for every idle word that comes out of our mouths" (Matthew 12:36). An idle word means a careless or non-beneficial word. [1]

Both Miriam and Aaron spoke and criticized their brother Moses, whom God had chosen. God was using Moses in great ways and his siblings were envious about it. Miriam said, "Does God only speak through Moses? Does He not also speak through us?" (Numbers 12:2 NIV). In other words, Miriam was bitter and felt that Moses was getting all the attention and appeared to be the only one that God seemed to use.

She felt that she should have the same right and felt that she should be able to get equal anointing. When God heard this, he was angry and told Miriam, Aaron, and Moses to come to the tent before Him for a meeting (Numbers 12). God said to Miriam, "There is no one humbler than your brother Moses on the earth and that is why I have used him and can speak to him face to face." God was so upset with Miriam that he struck her with leprosy for her careless words. The Bible says, "that God can hear every word we say," so that means we have to be careful with what comes out of our mouths.

There may be people in your own life that may have tried to discredit you or tried to bring you down in some way, but do not fret. Just as God defended Moses, God will take care of those who come up against you as well. Isaiah 54:17 says, "No weapon formed against us shall prosper and every tongue that rises against us in judgment will fall. Our job is not to pay people back for what they have said about us, instead, we are to give the problem over to God." Romans 12:19 says, "'Vengeance is mine, I will repay,' saith the Lord." God wants us to love those who hate us and bless those who curse us. [3] If people have

> Isaiah 54:17 says, "No weapon formed against us shall prosper and every tongue that rises against us in judgment will fall

spoken carelessly about you, then God will intervene on your behalf. God does not want anyone of us to allow unwholesome [foul, worthless, evil] talk to come out of our mouths. Instead, He wants us to use our words in ways that are helpful and can build others up. [4]

Over the years I have come to realize it is better to use my mouth for good things rather than the bad. I remember a time when I was very quick to speak my mind. Whatever I felt like saying, I would say. For example, if I was at work and felt that someone was not a good person, I would give my opinion without any forethought. This continued until one day a new friend of mine sent me a Bible verse on slander.

If you can imagine, I was shocked and embarrassed because I did not even realize that what I was doing was wrong. I was called out on my behavior by a friend who I felt was a woman of faith. I knew she had a close relationship with the Lord. She was pretty discrete and texted me a Bible verse instead of telling me point-blank what I was doing wrong. When I read the verse, it talked about slander. At that time, I did not even know what slander meant, so I had to look it up in the dictionary. I found out that slander meant making statements that could damage a person's reputation or speaking bad or evil against them. When I read this, I felt like crying. I came to the realization that I most likely slandered so many people in my life throughout the years, yet I was not fully aware that it was against God's word. I just thought it was normal for me to say whatever I felt like saying, when I felt like it, no matter how it would affect others. To be quite honest, I always remembered that friend and was grateful that she was caring and loving enough to help show me that I was wrong. It was at that point that I started evaluating what was coming out of my mouth. [2] Scripture tells us that people who think first and evaluate their words before speaking are wise, yet if they do not think before speaking they can cause more heartache in the end. [2]

1 Peter 3:10 says, "Whoever loves life and wants to see good days must keep their tongue from evil and their lips from deceitful speech." Often people think that the Bible is just a set of rules and regulations that we should

> *You are wise if you think before speaking*

follow. This is the farthest thing from the truth. Doing things God's way opens doors to blessings. This is what God wants us to have, to achieve the best life that He is ready and waiting to give us.

God gives us the Bible to help protect us from doing things that will harm us in the future and keep us from falling into Satan's pit. We can either use our words to build someone up or tear them down. When we say negative things, we open the door for the enemy to work in our hearts and our situation. However, if we use our words for good, we open the door to God that will allow us to bring love, hope, and healing to others.

Where the Mind Goes the Mouth Follows

Your mind is where it all starts, where your mind goes your mouth follows. The things that we think about and meditate on are what we end up saying as well. The mind is a very powerful thing. Proverbs 23:7 says, "For as the man thinketh so he is." This is plain and simple. God is saying to us, whatever we fill our minds with is what will come out of our mouths. If you think negative thoughts all day, you will naturally speak negatively. However, if you think positive thoughts you will speak more positively. The Bible says, "Think on things that are true, that are noble, that are just, that are pure, that are lovely, of good report and anything praiseworthy — meditate on these things" (Philippians 4:8). God wants us to think good thoughts, He wants us to focus on all the things that are right versus all the things that are wrong in our lives.

We can all find things that we are not happy with or focus on the sad things that may have happened to us. However, this does not do us any good. I am not saying that we are not to recognize our feelings, I am saying that we do not need to dwell on everything that is wrong with us. If we dwell on the negative all day long, it robs us of our joy and peace. [1] God gave us this illustration because He wants to show us that, yes, there may be things that can bring us down, but He wants us to keep our hearts and mind fixed on things above rather than below.

We cannot dwell on things that make us sad all day and expect to have joy. You cannot think and speak words of defeat and expect victory. I know of an older woman in my community who is somewhat debilitated; however, she can still cook, clean, and get around. Every time I would see her, she listed all her medical conditions from A-Z and told all the people around her that she was always sick. She went into detailed descriptions of each of her medical conditions and how they made her feel. She would say to those listening, "I now have arthritis, I cannot eat because of my bowel conditions, and I have to use this cane now." She went on and on, so that the others listening became discouraged as well.

Every time I heard this woman talk about how many problems she had, I started to feel down and disheartened just by listening to her. What was she doing? She was dwelling on her problems, which only magnified her issues. She was not expecting nor would be able to receive healing if she did not change her mindset and the words that were coming out of her mouth. You see, she was replaying the videotape of being sick, tired, and weak in her mind over and over again so that it became and continued to be her reality. Mark 11:23 (KJV) says,

"For verily I say unto you, that whosoever shall say unto this mountain, be thou removed, and be thou cast into the sea; and shall not doubt in his heart, but shall believe that those things which he saith shall come to pass; he shall have whatsoever he saith." This woman ended up having what she was saying. She continued to declare her sickness over and over again and unfortunately, she became more sickly over time.

Rather than speak our defeats, God says to use our words to declare victory! The Bible says, "Let the weak say I am strong" (Joel 3:10). So, we ought to say what God says and agree with His spoken words over us. He does not want you to make a list of everything negative about yourself, but rather make a list of all the good things that you have in your life. Jesus wants you to be courageous, rise, and say, "I can and do all things through Christ that strengthens me" (Philippians 4:13), and "If God is on my side of whom should I be afraid, if He goes before me then who can ever be against me!" (Romans 8:31). God wants you to rise beyond the muck, mire, and ashes and declare this is the day that the Lord has made, I will *rejoice* and be glad in it! (Psalms 118:24). We have all gone through many trials in our lives and the enemy would love for us to just give up and die. However, do the very opposite. Declare your victory in advance, speak it out, and expect God to do great things in your life!

Take Every Thought Captive

"Cast down imaginations, and every high thing that exalts itself against the knowledge of God and bring into captivity every thought to the obedience of Christ"
2 Corinthians 10:5 (NKJ).

Taking every thought captive means anything that comes to your mind that is not of God you should cast down, or in other words, "grab it and throw it down" and not allow it to enter your mind. It is important to know that every thought that comes to your mind is not of God, nor do you need to accept or entertain those thoughts.

Have you ever noticed that sometimes thoughts enter your mind and you have no idea how they got there? For example, you may have thoughts that God does not love you, you are not important, you are not accepted, or even as far as thinking you were meant to be a boy even though you were born a girl. These are thoughts that are opposite to God's word that the enemy tries to implant into our brain so that over time we will start to believe them. However, the Bible says that when the enemy whispers a thought in your mind that is contrary to God's word, you need to cast it down and shout a big NO! [1]

Growing up, thoughts would come into my mind that I knew were not of me. I recognized it was the enemy whispering lies into my ear. So, I would quickly and firmly declare, "No, devil, that is your thought and not mine. I will not agree with that thought and I command you to get out of my mind." The Bible says resist the devil and he will flee from you (James 4:7 NIV). The enemy will use anything he can to get us down if we let him. He throws fiery darts at us to steal our joy and peace and to cause us to lose hope. Satan puts thoughts into our minds and would love to throw us off course. He may put thoughts of doubt, hopelessness, loneliness, anger, and fear into us to get us to a place where we may want to turn away and reject others as well as God. I am sure that David must have felt the same way.

David was anointed by the prophet Samuel to be Israel's next king. He had just killed Goliath, with King Saul's permission, and won the battle. King Saul was very pleased with David when he won the battle and saved the Israelite army from death. However, once all the "women began to sing and declare that King Saul had killed thousands, but David his ten thousand" (1 Samuel 18:7), jealousy began to grow in King Saul's heart. David played the harp for King Saul to calm him of his tensions, anxiety, and fears. However, while he was playing, Saul, in jealousy, began to throw spears at David three different times but missed each time. By the third attempt, David ran from Saul. I am sure during his escape he had moments of hunger and thirst, and was tired. He ended up having to hide in a cave.

While in this cave he must have thought, "I was anointed and promised to be King one day, but look at me now. I am now hiding in a cave in fear of my life. what did I do? I was doing the right thing and the wrong thing happened. I did a good thing by defeating the

> Resist the devil and he will flee from you. James 4:7

mighty Goliath and saving the Israelites. I played music for King Saul and loved him and I never wanted to hurt him. Why has God allowed this to happen to me, where is He when I need Him?" I am sure the devil was having a field day by bombarding David's mind and causing him to doubt God.

However, David held on to his faith despite his feelings and put his focus on the Lord and took every thought captive and fought them with the word of God. King Saul found David in the cave, and God allowed David to have the upper hand; however, David chose to forgive King

Saul and not kill him when he had the chance. Instead, he decided to trust that God had him in the palm of His hands and was in complete control of his life. David had the right mindset and because of this, God decided to bless him even more.

Growing up, I never really understood that the enemy could implant thoughts of negativity in my mind and that I did not have to entertain it. I just figured that if a random thought came into my mind then it was something that I would need to dwell on and accept. Feelings of fear and worry bombarded my mind often and would take over my emotions. I felt powerless, but over time, the closer I became with the Lord, the more fear and worry had to subside.

If fear comes to my mind now, I know that I don't need to get on board with those thoughts, and I can say NO at its onset. If the thought that comes to your mind does not agree with the Bible, then it is not of God. That is why it is so important to read the word of God and know it for yourself, otherwise, the Devil can find ways to keep you bound up in chains.

This concept is also true of imagination. Let's say, for example, a person was diagnosed with cancer. If they allow it, the devil will show them pictures of their life ending and allow them to see their funeral and the people close to them crying around the casket. The enemy will try to fill your thoughts of every negative picture, even before it happens or it is proved true. We cannot allow our minds to be filled with imaginings or pictures of defeat even before we start the race. If you allow those imaginings and pictures of defeat to bombard your mind and not do deal with it at its onset, then the enemy can have a foothold in your life and bring you to destruction.

Rather than imagining yourself sick and defeated, begin to take action and start putting up pictures of you when you looked the best, the healthiest, the strongest, and start imagining yourself at that place again. Begin to pray about your needs and set it in front of you, persist in prayer, and begin to thank God for the answers to your prayers in advance. [2] God sees and hears you and will reward you for your persistence (Hebrews 11:6).

> *God sees and hears you and will reward you for your persistence (Hebrews 11:6).*

Use your words to talk to God openly about how you imagine your life to be. Speak words of life and victory and press into God's word and hold on to His promises! Take time to quote scriptures and remind yourself of God's promises. Keep knocking, asking, and seeking God for your needs that your joy would be made full and be complete (John 16:24). This is God's will and plan for you according to His word!

God's word helps us to understand how we can combat the lies of the enemy. The Bible is written to help us, prepare us, and give us the equipment needed to fight the principality and powers of darkness in this world. When the enemy talks to you, shoot him down quickly and tell him what God says about you! God has given you the power and victory to trample on the enemy's head and defeat him. [3] Hold on to every promise He has given you, resist and overcome the enemy, and declare your victory!

CHAPTER 6

Who Do You Say You Are?

Words are often a pretty good snapshot of what someone's character is like. We do not often realize it, but when we speak, we speak volumes about who we are and display our personality to those around us. What we say is often an indicator of what we have been meditating on or what is in our hearts. [1] When you speak, you are giving a detailed first impression of yourself to everyone you come in contact with. Whether you speak words that build others up or break them down, people who come in contact with you are gaining an understanding of who you are through your words.

Have you ever met a person for the first time and learned something about their character just from their conversations? Maybe they come off blunt, or they start off speaking foul language or are critical of others. The Bible says wise people analyze the words that they use, while others just simply say what comes out of their mouths without further thought. [2]

Matthew 15:18 says, "But those things which proceed out of the mouth come forth from the heart; and they defile the man." I have often struggled with being too blunt over the years and have made many mistakes of my own over time. However, I have come to realize that if I do not tame my tongue, I am only doing myself a disservice. It is better to take the time to evaluate what you are saying and think before speaking.

Take a moment to be silent and ask God for yourself what He feels needs changing; what does He bring to your mind? Is God speaking to you about an area in your life that needs to be changed? If so, join the club and humbly ask God to help make those changes within you. If you do this, you are working with God on becoming the best you can be. God's plans are for your good and He wants you to walk in victory. Our prayers should be, "Lord, let the words of my mouth and the meditation of my heart be acceptable in Thy sight, oh Lord, my strength and my redeemer" (Psalms 19:14). Let us all be the type of people that will come into agreement with God's plan and do the work that He wants to do in us. This may not always be easy, but I assure you, once He chisels away at the old and cuts off the things that do not produce fruit, you will be so much better off than where you used to be.

God wants to use you in greater ways than you can imagine. Let God fill your mouths with good things, words that bring life, hope, peace, love, and joy. Together, let us start making efforts to change the words that come out of our mouths by taking inventory of what we say, and ask for God's help every step of the way. As you grow in Christ and begin to take small steps and follow His

> *God's plans for you are good and he wants you to walk in victory.*

wonderful plan for your life, it is important to take some time and pat yourself on the back for making the changes in the areas of your life that God is showing you.

Put on the Full Armor of God

There may be people in your life that have spoken words of defeat, discouragement, and words that attempt to destroy you. However, the Bible says to put on the full armor of God, which includes the belt of truth, the helmet of salvation, shoes of peace, breastplate of righteousness, the shield of faith, and the sword which is the word of God (Ephesian 6:10-18 KJV). The sword is known to us as the Bible and is what we use to fight. To be able to fight opposition that comes your way, you need to be fully equipped for the battle and have the word of God within your heart that you can use when the enemy attacks you. To be able to fight the good fight of faith, it is important to memorize scripture and surround yourself with God's word. When you do this, your spirit man becomes stronger and stronger, to the point that the enemy's darts can no longer affect you.

> *To be able to fight the good fight of faith, it is important to memorize scripture and surround yourself with God's word.*

The Bible says we do not wrestle against flesh and blood, but against principalities, against powers, against the rulers of the darkness of this world, and spiritual wickedness in high places. We don't fight people necessarily, but we fight the evil powers that may be at work within them. Satan uses people to accomplish the work that he has hoped to destroy us with. So often what helps me to avoid being angry and bitter at someone that has hurt me is to turn it around and realize that this is a trick of the enemy to keep me in unforgiveness. He can cause us to be bitter and angry, which only holds us prisoner and causes the enemy to have a stronghold in our lives.

For example, when Satan brings a thought into my mind about someone that has hurt me and tries to get me stirred up, I say, "Satan, I am not going to hate that person who hurt me, because I know that is exactly what you want me to do. Instead, I will pray and forgive them, just like God has forgiven me when I make mistakes, and I will let God deal with them." When you do this, you have made a decision to combat evil with good, which is exactly what the enemy was hoping you would not do! (Romans 12:21 (NIV). I can imagine the enemy stomping up and down like a big baby saying, "NO, NO, NO, don't forgive them, just hate them... you are totally ruining my plans!!!" The enemy wants to destroy you and steal your peace and happiness, but don't let him!

Letting go of past hurts and forgiveness may not always be easy, but you must decide in your heart that you are going to do what God is asking you to do in His word. You must come to a place where you can say, "I will pray for that person, forgive them, and offer God's love and grace to them." The same kind of grace and forgiveness that God has given you and I when we make mistakes is what God requires that we do for others as well.

One day when I was spending time reading God's word and in prayer, God pointed me to the Lord's Prayer that was written in the Bible. He revealed to me that forgiveness is very important to him. It is so important that he decided to make it a part of our *daily* prayer. The daily prayer says, "forgive us our sins, as we have forgiven those who have sinned against us" (Matthew 6:12 NLT). This is so necessary, and the most important and vital step needed to have and maintain victory. You may have had a mother, father, friend, or another loved one speak negatively about you, but do not let it get inside of you. The devil will try his best to cause you to dwell on the negative remarks or actions that have come your way. He will try to tempt you to replay the videotape over and over again in your mind of what they have said or done to you, but don't fall for his tricks.

God has given you the power to be an overcomer and to overcome evil with good. We are only able to overcome the world and the powers of darkness by having faith in Jesus Christ (1 John 5:5). Jesus said, "Call on Me and I will answer you and show you great and mighty things of which you do not know" (Jeremiah 33:3). God is not against you, but for you. It is God's highest wish that you would prosper and succeed and be in health, even as your soul prospers. [1] Give all your years of brokenness, setbacks, hurts, and discouragement to God. Let Him handle the ones that have hurt you, and allow Him to deal with those that have caused you to be in pain.

> You are an overcomer and can overcome evil with good

God says in His word, "Instead of your [former] shame *you will have* a double *portion*; and *instead of* your humiliation and dishonor, your people will possess double [what they had forfeited]; and a double portion and inheritance of the land, so that everlasting joy will be theirs (Isaiah 61:7). This is powerful. God is saying that He will give you a double portion of that which has been taken from you. The enemy is the one who has come to steal from you, but God is the one who will restore you. God does not want us to pay people back by speaking hateful words, cursing, and being vile to those that have hurt us. Instead, He says to bless those that curse you and pray for those that have hurt you, so that you will inherit the wonderful blessing that He has for you. (see 1 Peter 3:9, Luke 6:28). God will deal with those who have hurt you. Commit your ways to God, trust in Him, and He will fight for you! [2]

The Word that Fell on Stony Ground

There were many people that surrounded Jesus when He spoke to them in parables. Jesus wanted to teach them about the love of God and all that was made available to them. He wanted to show them how they could have the best life now, and that life could be found in Him. He also taught them that the enemy of our souls will attempt to steal the life God has come to give them. Jesus has taught us that the enemy's plan is to come to steal, kill, and destroy, and bring us to a place of defeat. [1] That is why He has given us the word of God to remind us and continually point us to the truth.

There are many opportunities to hear God's words these days. We can hear about God through our television sets, the Internet, radio, and even come across statements about Christ when we are driving down the streets. It seems that the word of God is in plain view for all who want to receive from it. In Mathew 13, Jesus talks about the Parable of the Sower. He teaches that there are four kinds of soil that the seed can fall on. Now I want to emphasize that *Jesus* is known as the "sower," the *seed* is the "word of God" and the *soil* is how our "hearts" are represented.

Jesus tells us that a sower was sowing seed within his field and that life-producing seed was thrown into every direction. The seed that was thrown into the ground was meant to grow, become strong, and bear fruit. However, in the course of sowing the seeds, some fell onto a hard place and the birds came and ate it. This seed represents people who may hear the word of God, but because their hearts are hardened, maybe through pain, repeated suffering, or deep hurts, they reject God's love for them. However, what they may not know is that there is an enemy of their soul who wants to keep them in bondage, resentment, and in bitterness towards God.

The enemy uses other people to hurt us and bring about pain and suffering, yet tries to lie and fill our minds with unforgiveness so that we are stuck and unable to move forward. He comes to snatch the word of God out of our hearts before it takes root so that he can keep you and I down, defeated, and in bondage. The enemy knows that if that life-producing seed is watered and given sunshine - by reading and meditating on God's word - you will be able to grow, come alive, and bear fruit. (see Mathew 13:18-19).

The *second* type of seed that was sown fell on rocky ground. Often when people hear the word of God for the first time, they get excited and are ready to go. However, when the storms of life hit, and persecution comes their way, they are unable to stand because their roots did not go down deep but remained shallow. For our roots to go down deep, we have to cultivate and strengthen our foundation in the Lord by reading His word, surrounding ourselves with strong men/women of faith, and spending time in God's presence.

When you hear the word of God for the first time and are filled with joy because of the good news, don't stop there! Continue to water yourself, shine the light of the word,

> God looks out the window of heaven, smiles at you, and is rooting you on

and keeping growing, so that you can be all that God wants you to be, and reach your highest potential! (Matthew 13:20-21). God looks out the window of heaven, smiles at you, and is rooting you on. He is on your side and wants wonderful things for you, and that is why He encourages you to dig deep and plants your seeds in solid ground. When you do this, the enemy cannot uproot you. He stomps around in frustration, mad and yelling because now he knows he cannot keep you down and defeated. No, you are a child of the Most High God, and He wants you to rise, stand tall, and do all that He has called you to do!

The *third* type of seed fell on thorny ground. This is when people hear the word of God, yet the cares, distractions, deceitfulness of riches, and superficial (temporary) pleasures of this world choke out the word (Matthew 13:22). The enemy uses things to tempt us and lure us off the path that God has for us. It's almost like a person dangling a bone in front of a dog. That dog will grab that bone and chew it up if it is in the dog's view long enough. In the same way, the enemy studies us and knows what will catch our eye. He may use the love of a man or woman to get your eyes off of God, he may use pleasures, possessions, and power to distract you and get you off course, but don't let him! See, the enemy knows that the temporary pleasures of this world can never satisfy you as God can satisfy you. The Bible says that he is very cunning, the father of lies, and there is no truth in him (see John 8:44). He hopes to get you distracted so that you can no longer be focused on the things of God.

Have you ever noticed that when you sit down to pray, you suddenly start to think about all the things that you need to get done, or forgot to do? This again is a tactic of the enemy to distract you and keep you from focusing on God or the path that He has for you. If he can keep you distracted, he can keep you from making progress and being all that God has created you to be. The Bible instructs us to keep our eyes open, be sober-minded, and vigilant because the adversary - the devil - is a roaring lion that walks around and seeks whom he can devour (1 Peter 5:8). Yet, Jesus tells us to "seek ye first the kingdom of God and his righteousness and all these things shall be added unto us" (Matthew 6:33). God promises that if we keep Him first, then He will give us everything we need and supply all of our needs. When the enemy starts to whisper lies in your ear, don't underestimate the power of your words. Speak up, and combat his lies with God's truth!

The *fourth* and final type of seed fell on good soil. This seed was planted into a heart that was ready to receive God with everything that was within them. Once you hear the word of God it is important not to sit around waiting for the enemy to whisper doubts and lies into your mind. Instead, the Bible says, you ought to guard your heart with all diligence

Give and it shall be given to you

(Proverbs 4:23) to make sure you do not allow the enemy to steal the word from your heart. These people make attempts to understand God's word, make necessary changes, and grow in His truth.

The seed that takes root in good soil yields great crops, and this is the same for you and me. When the seed (the word of God) goes into your heart and you receive it, it will begin to take root, become strong, and produce amazing fruit. This fruit can bear thirty, sixty, or even a hundredfold harvest. It is God's will that we bear fruit and bear an abundance, but the choice is ours. If you consider yourself a strong Christian that is deeply rooted and planted in good soil, then you are ready to harvest your fruit. However, the return on your fruit is up to you. Whatever you sow, whether it be in areas of time, money, or the amount of faith you have to receive, is what you will receive in return.

Luke 6:38 says, "Give, and it will be given to you. A good measure, pressed down, shaken together and running over [with no space left for more], will be poured into your lap. For with the measure you use, it will be measured back to you in return. Our lack of faith can limit us from receiving all that God has for us." Matthew 21:21 says, "Truly I say to you, if you have faith and do not doubt, you will not only do what was done to the fig tree but even if you say to this mountain, 'Be taken up and cast into the sea,' it will happen".

Whatever a man sows is what he will reap (Galatians 6:7-9). God is saying we can do great things; however, we need to take action, and our responses will dictate our return. Take time to cultivate the seed within you and decide to bear a great harvest, as this is God's will for you. We all have the potential to receive a hundredfold return, but we must do something about it. Are you ready to receive the fruits of your harvest? If so, then get your empty baskets ready, start to speak in the direction you seek, and decide to take a step of faith to receive all that God has for you to receive.

SECTION II

MAKE CHANGES
THAT CAN MOVE
YOU FORWARD

CHAPTER **7**

We Are Accountable

Did you know that we are accountable for every word that comes out of our mouths? The Bible says that we are accountable to God in all things (Romans 14:12) and on the day of judgment we will need to give account for every careless word we speak. (Matthew 12:36). I don't know about you, but throughout my life, I have made several mistakes in these areas. There have been times that I have spoken ill of someone, criticized others, while thinking all along the way that I truly was not doing anything "that bad." However, I have to come to realize that the Bible is very clear on what God instructs us to do and that is to protect us from further heartbreak. It is our *Instruction Book* for life and it was given to us to follow, to guide us, and to offer us a wonderful life here on earth.

God's word teaches and shows us how to live the best life possible. I used to think that the Bible was a book full of rules; however, as I have taken time to slowly memorize scripture, I have come to realize it is God's word that is used to protect us and give us a life full of peace, love, and joy.

Idle Words

What are idle words? Idle words, according to Merriam Webster's dictionary, are words that are "not profitable, non-beneficial," or in other words, useless or careless words. Forms of idle words include statements like these: "I don't know 100% but I heard that..." "She failed the class because she's not that...," or "Look at the way he looks, he..." The Bible tells us in Ephesians 4:29, that we are not to let "any unwholesome talk come out of our mouths, but only what is helpful for building others up according to their needs, that it may benefit those who listen." Jesus is trying to communicate that he wants us to avoid evil talk or words that do not benefit others. [2] He does not want us to participate in slander, defaming others, or spreading gossip. James 1:26 says that those who consider

Life and death are in the power of your tongue

themselves religious and yet do not keep a tight rein on their tongues deceive themselves, and their religion is worthless.

As we know, in America, we are given the right to have freedom of speech. TV and social media have also allowed us to do the same; however, although we are given this wonderful privilege, it can also cause us to fall into a trap of speaking idle words. We as Christians are to heed God's warning to protect ourselves from destruction, as God has told us to not merely hear the word of God but to obey it (James 1:22). Our words have tremendous power that can offer life or death; however, we are accountable to God with whichever path we decide to choose.

Idle words are simply words that do not offer a benefit to anyone listening. Types of idle words include forms of gossip, grumbling, murmuring, or complaining. These types of words almost always stem from a source of contention or strife within our spirit. Gossip, according to the Miriam-Webster Dictionary, is "a person who repeats stories about other people or talks and spreads rumors about the personal lives of others." [1] The truth is, we are all guilty of this and can only strive to become better.

Typically, when we gossip or talk about someone in a negative light, it most often can come from a source of jealousy, bitterness, irritation, or strife. Gossip is often masked by saying things like, "I'm telling you this so you can pray for her." Or, "It was so crazy, but this happened to her..." Truly, what matters is the heart's motivation in what we say and what we do (Psalms 19:14). Often our lips move freely when we are talking about someone else's misfortune. However, if we were to put ourselves in that same situation, the question would then be if we would want someone to share our problems with others who are not in the absolute need to know?

Slander and gossip create division and strife among people and can separate the best of friends (Proverbs 6:28). Gossip hurts people and can defame the character of a person to others who may not know them well, or have not verified the facts of the rumor for themselves. Gossip is most often found in two forms - active and passive. Active gossip is when I share something that was personally confided to me, to another third party who has no business knowing what is being shared. The question you should ask yourself is, does this person need to know this information? Would the individual who has confided in me with this information be okay with me telling this third person? (Proverbs 17:9)

Passive gossip is where I join in on the conversation about others to offer my opinion or perspective without verifying the facts first. The truth is, it is often hard to find a setting, whether at work, school, or in different locations, that gossip is not heard. However, we do have a choice to either walk away, or not participate in the discussions. Just put yourself in that situation if you were the one being talked about. Would you want others to join in on the conversation, or choose not to say anything and not be a part of the discussions? Proverbs 13:3 says, "Those who guard their lips preserve their lives, but those who speak rashly will come to ruin."

Quite honestly, it is better to say nothing than to say something that you may regret. A rule of thumb that I use now is, would I say the same sentence to others if that person I was talking about was standing right in front of me? If no, then you and I ought to be more careful before we speak and keep a guard over our mouths (Psalms 141:3).

God does not want you to participate in conversations that can only lead you to trouble and more conflict. He says that we must avoid things like anger, rage, malice, slander, and filthy language from our lips" (Colossians 3:8). It is pretty amazing to me that God cares about what we think and what we say. Jesus wants to give us the best plan for our lives as we come into agreement with His plan for us.

> *God wants his children to walk in victory*

Grumbling, murmuring, and complaining (GMC) are also types of idle words. I heard a story of a young woman who was given a husband that was good and faithful to her. He may not have done everything 100% the way she wanted things, but he tried. Every day she would come home from work and find that he had not cleaned the dishes, the bathroom, or other areas around the house in the way she wanted things done. This went on for years, and eventually, her husband got tired of hearing her constant complaints and decided to leave her. He left saying, "I need some peace. I cannot live like this because you are driving me crazy!"

He eventually felt that life alone was better than living life with her, and unfortunately filed for divorce. With time he found another woman that valued him and was appreciative of what he was able to offer. I am saddened by his decision, but the truth is sometimes when we see the same blessings every day, we stop noticing them. And when we stop noticing the blessing, we become ungrateful and begin to grumble, murmur, and complain. This woman was given a great husband, but because she did not value him and noticed everything that was wrong with him, she ended up losing the very thing that she knew was a blessing to her.

In the same way, the Israelites were ungrateful to God and found everything that they were not happy about. Even though God had delivered the Israelites from slavery, and rescued them from Pharaoh's hand by dividing the Red Sea, they continued to grumble, murmur, and complain about everything. Shortly after leaving Egypt and walking through the desert, the Israelites began to complain to Moses and Aaron. They cried, "If only the Lord had killed us back in Egypt, we would not have to starve like this. There we sat around pots filled with meat and ate all the bread we wanted. But now you have brought us into this wilderness to starve us all to death" (Exodus 16 & 17).

God heard their complaints and said he would provide manna from heaven for them; however, over time their complaints grew even though God had met their needs.

Moses reminded them that their complaints were not against him and his brother Aaron, but their complaints were toward God. They then continued to complain because of thirst and were disgruntled rather than having a grateful attitude. Moses started to get annoyed by their constant complaints and shouted, "Quiet! Why are you complaining about me? And why are you testing the Lord?" Yet, the Israelites continued with their complaints.

Their complaints persisted and angered the Lord so much that it took them over 40 years to get to the promised land rather than the expected 11-day journey! All their GMC did not help the situation and only held them back from receiving all the blessings that God had desired to give them. In the end, it never pays to grumble, murmur, or complain. Instead, it is better to be humble and thankful for all that we receive, even the smallest of things.

Choosing our words carefully only helps and protects us from unwanted troubles. Having a heart of gratitude rather than GMC will lead us into the path that will bring us the most blessings. Ask God for His help in your areas of weakness and trust God to help you.

Choose to Have a Happy Life

The Bible says in 1 Peter 3:10-11, "If you want a happy and good life, keep your tongue under control and guard your lips from telling lies. Turn away from evil, do good, and run after peace." A happy life and good things do not come our way just by chance. It takes effort on our part.

We are partners with God, and when we partner with God and His word, we put ourselves in a position to be blessed. God is saying to you, "I love you, I have great plans for you, but if you want to participate in all that I have for you, come alongside me." God tells us that our mouths can get us in trouble, so we ought to maintain self-control, abstain from lies, and strive for peace in all things. Running after peace is not always easy, but is doable.

I struggled in my relationship with a relative who I felt had a harsh way of expressing herself. When this individual spoke, it would irritate me and I could feel my emotions rising. I have had my moments of confrontation; however, I knew it was not what God wanted me to do. I had to work very hard to strive for peace! I would talk to myself and say, "Julie, just calm down, lower your tone, don't engage and just walk away."

To be quite honest, this was very difficult to do. I had to pray that God would help me not to engage in an argument, even though my flesh wanted to rise and say what was on my mind. However, I knew that I needed to calm down and guard my mouth, so I did. I had to practice these steps over and over again until they were engrained in my heart. James 1:26 says, "If you claim to be religious but don't control your tongue, you are fooling yourself, and your religion is worthless."

> *The word of God is alive and active and helps to show us how to have the best life now.*

We all face moments where we lose our cool; however, a wise person uses self-control. The Bible says, "He who guards his mouth and his tongue guards himself against troubles because too much talk will lead to sin" (Proverbs 21:23; Proverbs 10:19). The Lord knows that the more our tongue moves, the quicker it is to enter into conflict, and that is why He tells us to tame our tongues. Jesus wants the best for us. The word of God is alive and active and helps to show us how to have the best life now. Philippians 4:9 says, "Whatever you have learned or received or heard from me, or seen in me, put it into practice. And the God of peace will be with you."

"He who heeds the word wisely will find good, and whoever trusts in the LORD, happy is he"
Proverbs 16:20 (NKJV)

When we put the word of God into action or practice and do what God instructs us to do in His word, we position ourselves to receive victory. Proverbs, among many other books in the Bible, is full of wisdom and instruction that help guide and teach us how to live our best life now. Many times, people read the Bible as if it is a storybook; however, the Bible is the living word of God by which we need to live our life.

Keep the Peace

Years had passed by and neither of them was talking to each other. After all, Jacob had cheated his brother out of his entitled birthright and his father's blessing. Jacob even went as far as disguising himself so that his father, who had difficulty seeing, would be deceived into thinking that Esau was receiving the blessing, when in fact it was Jacob.

Esau had every right to be angry at his brother. His brother deceived and stole what rightfully belonged to him. After his father told him that his brother Jacob had deceitfully stolen his blessing, Esau became angry. He started to lash out and said to himself, "The days of mourning for my father are near; then I will kill my brother Jacob" (Genesis 27:1). He was angry with his brother even to the point of wanting to kill him. Esau's mother Rebekah heard what Esau said, and she told her son Jacob to flee.

For years the two brothers were apart because of the pain that was created between them. Esau had the choice of forgiving his brother for the offense and could have allowed God to handle his affairs, but he let his anger get the best of him. He allowed the anger to get rooted in his heart. It was only with God's help that he was able to forgive and eventually make peace with his brother.

When people hurt us, we do not have to fall for the tricks of the enemy, because we know he is a thief that comes to steal our peace and our joy. However, you must decide in advance not to allow the enemy to take what rightfully belongs to you. Otherwise, he gladly will! There are many areas in which we can keep strife out of our lives and maintain our peace. However, the two that Esau and Jacob dealt with mostly were anger and unforgiveness.

We all have become angry at one point or another, and this is a part of our human nature. It is not wrong to be angry, but it is how we express the anger that can get us into trouble. Often when we get angry, we feel like giving someone a piece of our mind.

Take a moment and think before speaking

We want to say whatever we feel like saying and do whatever we feel like doing; however, the Bible advises us differently. Ephesians 4:29

(AMP) says, "Do not let unwholesome [foul, profane, worthless, vulgar] words ever come out of your mouth. Instead only such *speech* that is good for building up others, according to the need *and* the occasion, so that it will be a blessing to those who hear [you speak]." This may feel hard to do at the moment, but it will keep you out of trouble.

Often, we say things that we regret, whether it be with our spouse, parents, children, or any other relationship that we are in. Rather than blurting out your feelings, decide to take a moment, calm down, and breathe before you speak. What you say in a quick moment can be remembered for a lifetime, so make sure to control your tongue and maintain your cool. Proverbs 29:11 NKJV says, "A fool vents all his feelings, but a wise *man* holds them back. A person with understanding has patience, is not quick-tempered, and overlooks offenses." [1]

Offenses will always come our way, whether it be through insults, criticism, gossip, or slander. However, God says that He does not want us to repay evil for evil, insult with insult. Instead, repay evil with blessing so that we can inherit our blessings. God is just and does not want us to take matters into our own hands, rather He said He will avenge us and deal with those who have wronged us. (1 Peter 3:9, Romans 12:18-19).

The enemy's plan is to create division and strife and steal your peace. [2] The next time you feel like arguing with your spouse or someone in your life, imagine that there is a demon sitting on the couch between the two of you, trying to stir the anger and working hard to create division. If he can accomplish this, he can destroy you, your home, your marriage, and ultimately your children.

This is what it means when the Bible says, "You are not fighting against *flesh and blood,* but against rulers, against the authorities, against the powers of this dark world and the spiritual forces of evil in the heavenly realms" (Ephesians 6:12). The next time you are tempted to give someone a piece of your mind, stop, ask for God's help, follow His advice in the Bible, and He will come through for you, just as He has promised.

Similar to anger, unforgiveness can also be a huge peace stealer. Unresolved anger can lead to unforgiveness, years of misery, and heartache. If someone has hurt you or inflicted great pain in your life in one way or another, it is very tempting to hold on to that bitterness, resentment, and unforgiveness. This is exactly what the enemy would love for you to do. He knows that if you hold on to unforgiveness this will block you from freely fellowshipping with the Lord.

The Bible says that if you are not able to forgive others of their sins then God cannot forgive you of your sins (Matthew 6:14-15). You may say, "Well, you do not know what happened to me," or "My ex-spouse caused me so much pain and heartache." However, God sees everything that you have been through and He has promised to fight your battles as you continue to trust Him.

Many people do not realize that forgiveness is not for their sake, rather it is for your own sake. Unforgiveness keeps you bound in chains and strongholds that can poison your life. Just like stress can physically affect your body, unforgiveness can do the same. Unforgiveness can lead to depression, anxiety, mood swings, and cause increases in stress levels and blood pressure that can then lead to even deeper health conditions.

We may always run into issues of someone who offends us in some shape or form, but I have learned that letting go of the offense immediately or at its onset helps prevent it from taking root within my spirit. In other words, when others hurl insults or criticize you, let the offense slide right off of you and don't allow it to stick. God instructs us to bear with one another, forgive others when they make mistakes, just as God forgives us when we make mistakes, whether it is big or small (Colossians 3:13).

Jesus understood this when He died on the cross. He was an innocent man who had done no wrong. Yet His people mocked, betrayed, criticized, tortured, and persecuted him, though He did not sin against them. Instead, He cried out to His Father and said, "Father, forgive them, for they do not know what they are doing" (Luke 23:34). Jesus felt our pain, yet even still knows that we would be hurting ourselves by keeping the anger and unforgiveness within rather than letting it go.

> *Unforgiveness can keep us from receiving God's best for our lives*

I have gone through my share of troubles and offenses. I held on to hurts, insults, and things that were done to me, but one day when I was spending time reading God's word, I came upon the passage about praying the Lord's Prayer. The prayers spoke about "forgive us our trespasses, as we have forgiven those who trespass against us; and lead us not into temptation, but deliver us from evil [or: the evil one]. For thine is the kingdom, the power, and the glory forever and ever, Amen" (Matthew 6:9-13). While reading this passage, it dawned on me that God felt that forgiveness was so important that he felt the need to include it in our *daily* prayer.

I meditated on this for a while and realized that if I did not forgive others of their sins against me, then God could not forgive me. I apologized to the Lord right there in my living room and asked God to help me not to be tempted and to deliver me from the evil one who attempted to keep me bound in chains. I decided that day to forgive those who had hurt me and hand my hurts over to the Lord.

If the enemy has kept you wrapped in chains and bondages for years, decide to let the offense go and disarm the enemy by choosing forgiveness. Get rid of all bitterness, rage, anger, harsh words, and slander. Instead, be kind to each other, tenderhearted, forgiving one another, just as God through Christ has forgiven you (see Ephesians 4:31-32). Forgiveness is a choice and not a feeling. As you make a decision you will begin to take the first step toward walking in freedom and God's victory in every area of your life!

CHAPTER 8

God's Ears are Open to Your Prayers

To live a happy life, it is important to live in love, maintain peace, be kindhearted and humble in spirit. When we live according to God's standards, we open the door for His blessings. Often people wonder why things are not going their way, but when we take time to obey God and do as He instructs us to do, we can expect great things! The Bible says, "God's eyes are on the righteous and his ears are open to their prayers" (1 Peter 3:12). So, when people have chosen to hurt you in some way, whether it be in word or deed, God sees this and will take the matter into His own hands. [1] You can rest assured that God is a God of justice and He will compensate you for the years that you have lost and what has been stolen from you.[3]

I believe this with all my heart. When others hurt us with their words or actions we don't have to go to their level and pay them back. When we live by following God's

85

word, He puts a hedge of protection around us and saves us in our time of need (Psalms 33: 18-22). However, when we do things against His word and His advice to us, we open the door to the enemy, who wants us to remain in a spirit of unforgiveness, hatred, and bitterness.

A good man produces good things out of the treasure of his heart and an evil man, evil things from out from his heart. [2] Basically, what's on the inside of us will eventually come out with time. [4] Haman was a man that we find in the Bible who had an evil heart. He wanted to destroy the Jewish people because he was irritated by one man named Mordecai. Haman was the chief advisor to King Xerxes of Persia, and he was a proud man who demanded obedience and worship from those beneath him. When Mordecai, a Jewish man, refused to bow down before him, Haman became infuriated. He wanted to seek revenge, so he convinced the King to pass a new law that would annihilate the Jewish race. Talk about someone who has an evil heart! I mean, this man was malicious because he tried to convince the King to kill all Jews on account of one Jew that he did not like.

However, when Mordecai, along with the other Jews, heard the plan Hamman had orchestrated, they began to mourn and fast in sackcloth and ashes. Mordecai, who was Queen Esther's uncle, met with her in secrecy and told her she needed to do something about Haman's vicious plan. He said, "Do not think that you will be spared from this, just because you are in the King's Palace, for you are also a Jew." He then went on to say, "Maybe God had put you in this position as queen for such a time as this and to protect the Jewish nation from being destroyed" (Esther 4:13-14). Mordecai's words called his niece Esther to action! He described the seriousness of the issue and pleaded with her to do something.

Esther was torn on what to do because it would be a risk to speak to the King without his permission. However, she determined with resolve to attempt to meet with the King even if it meant death. As she stated in Esther 4:16, "If I perish, then I perish." Mordecai's words helped to influence a change within her heart which was necessary to save their nation. Esther, with her Uncle's words of encouragement, decided to take a stand on behalf of her people no matter what the cost would be.

I thought this was pretty amazing. Mordecai spoke words that caused his niece to rise up and do something about a situation that could save millions. Your words can have the same power on those around you. Decide to make a choice today that will breathe life into your family, causing them to rise higher and become all that they can be.

Avoiding Pitfalls

The only way to avoid pitfalls with your words is to truly take a moment and think to yourself about what you are going to say. When you speak, do your words build up or benefit the person that hears them? Or do your words bring contention, anger, or cause hurt? Something that has always helped me before I speak is to think about what Jesus would say. I know this may sound like a cliché, but it truly does help us at the moment and reminds us of what we ought to do. If you ever come across a situation in your life, regardless of what it may be, it is a good idea to say, "What ought I to do in this situation, or what should I do?" This will help guide you towards the right path. As long as we do the "right" thing we can be assured that God agrees with that choice of doing what we know we ought to do. [1] God gives us a step-by-step approach on how to deal with conflict rather than doing things our way.

For example, if your brother or sister sins against you or wrongs you in some way, the Bible instructs you to go and point out their faults, just between the two of you. If they listen to you, you have won them over. However, if they do not give you a listening ear, then take two or three witnesses with you to help discuss the issue (Matthew 18:15). This passage does not say that we are to discuss the problem with 10 people, but rather discuss our issues or hang-ups with the person privately. This is God's way of dealing with a problem and it helps keeps us out of trouble. Gossiping and talking bad about someone are things which we all are guilty of (Ephesians (4: 29-31). However, there are some things that we can do to protect ourselves.

Helpful Tips:

Think before speaking. Be aware of what you are saying and take a moment to pause before you open your mouth to ask yourself if there will be any consequences for what you will say. [3]

1. Clear communication - Try to clearly communicate what you are attempting to say. Trying your best in this area can only help you and not hurt you.

2. Only say what you can prove - Be careful that you are not saying something that you think happened

or what you have concluded based on what you have heard.

3. Do not say what you think you know - You may think you know the whole story about someone's life just by looking at them, but this can be farthest from the truth. God has advised us not to judge or slander anyone. Instead, our job is to love others, the Holy Spirit's job is to convict people, and the Father's job is to judge them [2] (Matthew 7:1-5). I don't know about you, but I am so glad that my only job is to love others and let God do the rest.

4. Walk away - When you come across people who often slander, gossip, and complain, it is best to avoid them. Do not hang around those that you know and feel in your spirit are not good to be around (Proverbs 20:19). The spirits within us are transferable and we can rub off on each other. Most often we can see that hanging around those that are angry can also cause you to be angry. Hanging around those that are positive will naturally cause you to be positive. Surround yourself with people that inspire you and cause you to rise higher.

5. Do the right thing - this is pretty plain and simple. Doing the right thing is what we ought to do and what Jesus instructs us to do (1 Thessalonians 5:15). This may seem difficult, but it keeps us from destruction and allowing the enemy to use us as a tool to hurt others. Slander, criticism, gossip, and strife are not what God calls us to do because it inhibits us from having the best life possible that He has made available for us.

Before you choose to slander, lie, or gossip just think, *if Jesus were standing in front of me, what would I say or do?* God wants the best for each of us and he does not want us to fall into the enemy's trap. He gave us His word to protect us from harm and keep us on the right path. God wants us to be victorious so that you and I can live a life that we love. A life that brings us joy, peace, and every good thing. [4]

Think and Talk about Good Things

The Bible says that we ought to think about good things. Philippians 4:8 says "Finally, brothers and sisters, whatever is true, whatever is noble, whatever is right, whatever is pure, whatever is lovely, whatever is admirable — if anything is excellent or praiseworthy —

> *Philippians 4:8 says "Finally, brothers and sisters, whatever is true, whatever is noble, whatever is right, whatever is pure, whatever is lovely, whatever is admirable — if anything is excellent or praiseworthy — think about such things and the God of peace will be with you."*

think about such things and the God of peace will be with you." Whatever we think about is what we end up talking about. Often we think that whatever comes to our mind is what we ought to accept and meditate on. However, you have control over what you think about. You do have the choice to take that thought captive, which means to recognize it, hold it, and bring it down (2 Corinthians 10:5 KJV). Or you can choose to dwell on the thought and allow it to become bigger and bigger so it steals your joy and peace.

We have the power to block and say NO to every thought that is against the word of God. The enemy tries to bombard our minds with thoughts that are not godly nor consistent with God's word. He tries to whisper words of criticism, condemnation, and lies. He also tries to infiltrate our minds with thoughts of fear, worry, and every negative thought that we often deal with. However, we do not have to accept these negative thoughts, and with the power of Jesus Christ, we have the authority to tear down these strongholds.

I once heard a story of a woman who was diagnosed with a terminal condition. She desperately wanted to be healed and did everything in her power to pursue that healing. She prayed, fasted, attended healing services, read scriptures aloud, and put pictures of herself around her room that reminded her of a time when she was healthy and strong. [1] This woman was trying her very best to talk to God about living and she did not feel that she was ready to die. However, the enemy would try his very best to get her down and discouraged. He would bring thoughts of her lying at her own funeral service, and then posed the question of what outfit she should wear? One day this thought came again ,and while lying in her bed she began to look at her closet of clothes and think about what outfits she would look best in. [1]

At the time she did not recognize that this was the voice of the enemy, and so she began to engage in thinking about what she should wear to her funeral. She even went as far as to try to figure out which color would look the best on her. She eventually came to the understanding that this was a trick of the enemy to get her to engage in negative thinking, discouragement, and doubt. She later learned that this is what it means to take every thought captive and cast down "imaginations" that are not of God. [1] The enemy displayed a picture in her mind of all the negative things that had already happened to her, the funeral service, and everyone mourning her death. However, this was farthest from the truth!

As a result of casting down imaginations and taking every negative thought captive, she was able to overcome this wrong thinking. The Bible says in 2 Corinthians 10:5, *"Cast down imaginations, and every high thing that exalts itself against the knowledge of God, and bring every thought into captivity to the obedience of Christ."* The Bible is the ruler by which we should measure our life and it guides us into all truth. With much prayer, support, and determination, this woman was able to overcome her terminal diagnosis and continues to live 36 years later! Is there a picture or image in your mind that the enemy is continually putting before you that has no scriptural basis.? Does he plant thoughts in your mind that are opposite to God's word? When we engage in wrong thinking, we eventually engage in speaking words of doubt, fear, worry, and defeat. The enemy may try to bring you down; however, you have the spiritual authority to defeat him! Take your stand, be alert, guard your mind, and trust God to help you.

> *The Bible is the ruler by which we should measure our life and it guides us into all truth*

Be Quick to Listen and Slow to Speak

For most of us, listening versus speaking can be a very difficult thing to do. However, the Bible teaches us that we must be quick to listen and slow to speak, which can be a hard concept for most people to grasp. Many of us want to be able to speak our minds, say what we want to say, and express ourselves in whatever form we would like to. We often listen to quickly respond and offer our opinion, rather than listening to understand a person's opinion or side of the story. This was the case when the Pharisees came across a woman who had committed adultery.

When some of the religious scholars and Pharisees found out what she was doing, a great crowd gathered around her and quickly came to Jesus and said that they had found this woman caught in the very act of committing adultery. In their righteous anger, they felt the boldness to be able to come before Jesus, cast judgment, and ridicule her for her sins. "Teacher," they said to Jesus, "this woman was caught in the very act of adultery. The law of Moses says to stone her. What do you say?" (John 8 1-11 NLT). They were trying to trap Jesus into saying something that they could use against Him, but Jesus stooped down and began to write in the dust with His finger.

In his calm demeanor, without listening to their shouting, cursing, and snide remarks, he began to write slowly in the dust. I am sure that the Pharisees were infuriated that Jesus was not answering them quick enough. They wanted him to give them an answer right away. They did not want to listen to a voice of reason, quiet their hearts, nor evaluate their own lives. They were also not interested in wanting to gently correct her with compassion and humbleness. Instead, they demanded a quick answer from Jesus and did not want anyone to tell them they were wrong in their approach. With their increasing demands, Jesus stood up and said, "All right, but let the one who has never sinned throw the first stone!" Then he stooped down again and wrote in the dust one more time (see John 8:8).

I am sure the Pharisees were annoyed that Jesus was gentle, not quick to take their side and listen to their complaints. He listened and was slow to speak. When the accusers heard Christ's requests, they slipped away one by one, beginning with the oldest, until only Jesus was left in the middle of the crowd with the woman." On the ground, Jesus may have written, "You lied to your friend - I had mercy on you. You killed your brother - I had mercy on you. You fornicated with that woman - I had mercy on you," and so on.

Although we are not exactly sure what Jesus wrote in the dust, it was enough to quiet the religious scholars and help them understand that they too had made mistakes that needed mercy and forgiveness. They were quick to offer their input and judge her, rather than taking the time to think wisely and take inventory of their own lives.

Once the Pharisees scattered, Jesus said to the woman, "Where are your accusers? Didn't even one of them condemn you?" "No, Lord," she said. And Jesus said, "Neither do I, go and sin no more." (See John 8). Jesus showed her compassion and forgiveness. As Christians we cannot *hate* people to Christ, rather we can *love* them to Christ. We will never be able to get a non-believer to follow Christ through hate, criticism, condemnation, and judgment. However, people are more receptive to making changes in their lives when they are gently guided with love, compassion, and forgiveness, just as Jesus has demonstrated to us. Jesus took the time to be patient, He listened to her, spoke with wisdom, and "gently" guided her on the right path.

> *We can use our words to build others up or bring them down*

Our words can offer healing to those that are hurting all around us.

When you are alone you can simply pray, "Lord, help me to be quick to listen and slow to speak. Help me to love people to Christ and look at them through the lens of Jesus Christ rather than the lens of judgment, hate and criticism." God will help you do this, as you are sensitive and receptive to the Holy Spirit's leading. We have the option of using our words to build others up or bring them down. Let us follow Christ's example and offer love to those who are hurting and in need of an encouraging word. If you are willing God can use you to help mend the broken hearts that are surrounding you. Ask God how you can help and He will show you.

CHAPTER 9

Change Your Perspective

What is perspective, anyway? Perspective means our attitude, our point of view or outlook on things. [1] Do you find that you are often optimistic or pessimistic? When you are going through a situation do you often look at the bright side of things or do you only focus on the downside? I heard a story of two shoe salesmen who were sent to a remote part of Africa to look for a business opportunity. One man sent a telegram home that said: "Quick, honey, get me home, nobody here wears shoes, I cannot sell anything!" The other salesman's telegram said: "Quick, honey, send me all of the shoes you can, nobody here wears shoes. I can sell to the whole country!" [2]

It is easy to look at all the negative things that can often surround us. However, the truth is that we all go through situations and problems in our lives, but it is how we look at them that can make all the difference. In the story above, we see two men that were faced with a problem. However, one man looked at his problem and saw all the things that were negative and impossible, while the other man looked at the same problem and was positive, hopeful, and saw all the possibilities.

All kinds of things can happen in our lives. The unpredictability and challenges of our lives can make it very difficult to know what may come our way. However, our attitude and outlook can make all the difference in the world.

When I have faced difficulties, I have often reminded myself that I have two choices. I can either become stressed and let the problem overcome me, or I can look for the good in the situation and trust God to keep me. Even if you are going through the darkest of times, keep your thoughts above and not below because there is always a light at the end of the tunnel. The Bible instructs us to fix our thoughts on what is true, honorable, right, pure, lovely, admirable, excellent, and worthy of praise (Philippians 4:8).

This is what God is asking for us to do to overcome any obstacles that we face. To be quite honest, I love this verse and try to practice it to the best of my ability. When I'm at work, I purposely choose to focus on all the things that are going right in my life versus focusing on what's going wrong. We have to admit that when we think about good things, it makes us smile, feel light-hearted and happy. However, when we think about what's not working or going well in our lives, we appear more worried, discouraged, and distraught. Which of the two is better? Which one would you rather be? This is exactly what took me many years to learn.

I grew up always focusing on the negative things, being worried about my exams, my future and where I was headed. However, now I have realized that worrying and focusing on my problems did not help me one bit. It did nothing for me and did not solve my problem, but just made things worse. It is hard to enjoy your life when you are so burdened with the cares of life. Satan may bring trouble your way, cause suffering, or try to bring you down, but don't let him. Keep your head up, pull your shoulders back and declare that you are a child of God!

Use your words to declare what God's word says about you and your situation. There may be things that you cannot control, but focus on the things that you can control. I believe that is why God gave us these verses in the Bible to remind us to keep our eyes fixed on Him. When the enemy tries to discourage you, use God's word and declare that you are more than a conqueror through Jesus Christ who loves you (See John 8:37).

Joseph was a key example of someone who suffered unjustly. He was thrown into a pit by his brothers although he was innocent, and sold as a slave to Potiphar, the Captain of the Palace guard (Genesis 37-39). Joseph, after serving Potiphar with integrity and excellence, was lied about and accused of rape by Potiphar's wife, thrown in jail, and left forgotten by others. Yet it is admirable to me that he did not ball up a fist towards God and become resentful and angry. Instead, he remained humble and kept a good attitude.

Keep your eyes on Jesus and he will bring you through

I believe this is one of the reasons that God promoted Joseph to become second in command of Egypt. God knew Joseph's heart, and even though he was faced with the hardest of circumstances he consistently remained hopeful, faithful, and of sound mind. When we keep our minds fixed on the Lord, it keeps us joyful and prevents us from getting down and depressed no matter what our circumstances are. Satan will do his very best to prevent you from reaching your full potential, but God is there to protect us as we follow His lead. The Bible instructs us to "always be joyful and never stop praying, and be thankful in all circumstances for this is God's will for us who belong to Christ Jesus" (see 1 Thessalonians 5:16-18).

You know, when I first read this verse, I was surprised that this was the way that God wanted me to act no matter what I was facing. It helped me to realize the attitude that God expects us to have amid our struggles. Even though I was going through tough circumstances, I knew it was the Lord's will for me to remain steadfast and trust in him for my deliverance. This changed my perspective on how I was to live life. In reading the word I discovered the way God wanted me to think about problems, and how He wanted me to lean on Him by trusting Him in every circumstance, which is what He wants from all of us.

Being joyful in all circumstances took me some time to learn. At first, when I went through difficulties, I focused on the problem so intently that it stole my joy and caused me to become worried and distressed. However, when I started realizing that my situation was not going to change whether I was happy or miserable, that's when I decided to make some changes. My negative attitude was not going to make a difference in my situation, so I knew I needed God's help. God was willing to help me if I was willing to let go and allow Him to lead me through my situation.

Even though I was going through the darkest of times, I would wake up and say, *"This is the day that the Lord has made, I will rejoice and be glad in it."* (Psalms 118:24). Or, *"I can do all things through Christ who strengthens me"* (Philippians 4:13). This is what God wants of us daily. No matter what we go through, He has said that He will never leave us nor forsake us, and we are in the palm of His hands. Every day, we can wake up and make these declarations over our lives. Your words have power, so use them to declare your victory!

Count your Blessings

> A thankful heart, it opens the door for God to be able to bless us.

No matter what you go through or how dark your storm may be, there is always something that you and I can be grateful for. We can be grateful that we have a roof over our heads, food to eat, children, family and friends to love, or anything that brings us joy. There is always something to be grateful for, and this attitude is what honors and pleases God. When we have a thankful heart, it opens the door for God to be able to bless us. God wants to bless us with more; however, our ungrateful spirit can keep us from receiving God's best for our lives.

This was the problem with the Israelites. Even though they were given so much they continued to grumble, murmur, and complain. Moses became so fed up by their behavior that he scolded them by saying, "Your complaints are not against me but God." The Israelites were focused on what they did not have, rather than focusing on the blessings that God had already given them (Exodus 16:8). Their grumbling and ungrateful spirit prevented

God from being able to bless them. God wanted to bless them in great ways; however, their attitude and constant complaints were what kept them from receiving God's very best for them.

What was meant to be an 11-day journey to get to the promised land instead became a 40-year walk in the wilderness! The Israelites were so focused on what they did not have, they could not see the very blessing they already had. Often, we can become so down and focused on the problems that we are not able to see the wonderful things that God has done for us. The enemy wants us to stay focused on the negative things in our lives. If we are caught up and so focused on the negative, we become too busy to focus on the positive or the good things that God has already done for us.

If you think about it realistically, being negative and having a poor attitude does nothing for you and me. So, we might as well have a good attitude and look at things in the best way possible so we can enjoy our life, right here and right now. Jesus always looked at people from a different perspective. He looked at people through the eyes of love and mercy rather than with condemnation and hatred. This is seen when Jesus was invited to a Pharisee's home. He was sitting at a table when a woman from the local town heard about him and came to see him. She was a sinful woman and began to cry when she saw him.

As she stood behind him at his feet weeping, she began to wet his feet with her tears. She then wiped his feet with her hair, kissed him, and poured perfume on his feet. When the Pharisee who had invited him saw this, he said to himself, "If this man were [really] a prophet, He would know who is touching Him and what kind of woman she is, He would know what kind of terrible sinner she is (Luke 7: 39).

Jesus instantly knew his thoughts and gave him this example. He said, "Simon, if two people owed money to a money lender, with one man owing $500 and the other $50, but the money lender decided to forgive them both of their debts, who do you think would be the most remorseful, thankful, and more abounding in love for the forgiveness?" Simon said, "The one with the most debt, I suppose." Jesus said, "You have judged correctly. This woman knew she was a sinner and she was not hiding that fact. She was so sorry for her sins and asked for forgiveness to the point that she wet my feet with her tears and wiped them with something valuable to her, her [expensive] perfume (Luke 7)."

Jesus then proceeds to say to Simon, "Do you see this woman? I came into your house. Yet, you did not give me any water for my feet, but she wet my feet with her tears and wiped them with her hair. You did not kiss me (customary to normal practice) but this woman, from the time I entered, has not stopped kissing my feet. You did not put oil on my head (like our custom instructs us to do), but she has poured perfume on my feet. So, Simon, her sins, which are many, are forgiven, because she loves me much; but he who is forgiven little loves little." (Luke 7:44-45). Jesus then looked at the women and said: "Your sins are forgiven." She then went away praising God for His goodness (Luke 7:48).

I love this about Jesus! He looks at people from a different perspective. Simon wanted to condemn and judge this woman, but God saw her heart, and even though she committed many sins that caused her to burst out in tears, God forgave her of them all. God looks at both you and me with the same eyes of love and forgiveness, which we are to be so grateful for. We have the opportunity and privilege to be able to have a relationship with a good and loving God. He has done so much for every one of us, and we ought to take the time to talk to Him openly, freely from our hearts, and tell Him how much He means to us.

God Can Transform You

"Do not copy the behavior and customs of this world, but let God transform you into a new person by changing the way you think." (Romans 12:2 (NLT))

God wants to renew your mind and help you to be all that you can be. He has given you His master plan on how this can come forth. When we read God's word and put the word of God within us, we can grow in leaps and bounds. God unfolds His plan for our lives through the pages of His word. If we try to change ourselves without His help, we most likely will fail. However, the wonderful thing is that He is there to help us through the process. The Bible is truly a gift from God because it teaches us how to look at life from His perspective and live according to His best plan for us.

When our mind changes, our mouth changes. Your mind and your mouth are in sync. That is why we truly have to pay attention to what we put in our minds, because it will affect what we do and say. God helps us to understand this more clearly in His word.

> *When our mind changes our mouth changes*

103

Growing up as a young child in church, I felt that I understood the Bible pretty well, and I knew most of the stories from the sermons that I had listened to. I figured that I pretty much knew everything that I needed to know, so I did not take time to read the whole Bible for myself. I used to only read sections of the Bible that made me feel good, like Psalms, Ephesians, Philippians, and so on. However, I never really ventured off beyond this because I did not feel I needed to.

You see, at that time things were going very well for me. I was young, had no major problems, was healthy, and so I felt content not having to search for God beyond the chapters that I loved to read. However, it was when I faced the trials in my life that were beyond my control that I opened the Bible and desperately began to seek what God wanted me to do. While reading the Bible I knew that I had missed out on so much wisdom, knowledge, and understanding over the years because I had limited myself to the pages that made me feel good.

When I faced difficulties in my life, I did not know how to truly get out of them or get the help I needed. I used to cry and say, "God, please tell me what You want me to do in this situation! I need to hear from You. Just tell me what direction I need to go in, and I will obey You!" However, what I did not realize was that I had the answers right in front of me but disregarded it. I had the Bible, the living word of God, which is God's voice and words to us, right in front of me, but I did not realize it.

I feel pretty embarrassed to say this, but I used to think that reading the entire Bible was something that you did when you got old, but not something that you did when you were young. Boy, was I wrong! When I opened the

Bible and started reading from Genesis to Revelation, I learned so much about God and the great plan that He wanted to give me. I heard about stories of people who endured hardships even though they trusted God, yet He was with them and led them through the darkness. I then began to learn about the love of Christ and His compassion and thoughts toward every one of us.

This changed my perspective and helped me to realize that God was not someone who was trying to beat me over the head with a bat for everything that I did wrong. Instead, His arms were open wide to me despite my shortcomings and my failures. I realized that the Lord was trying to give me instructions on how to make the best decisions for my life

> His arms were open wide to me despite my shortcomings and my failures.

through His words. While reading, God was giving me revelation on the mistakes I had made, and showed me what I needed to change, and the great life He wanted to give me if I did things His way.

If we want to hear God's voice, we can do this by reading the Bible and using wisdom. I'm not saying that this is the only way to hear from God, but when you think you have heard from Him, take a step to make sure His word to you matches what the Bible has to say about it. Sometimes people don't want to believe that hearing from God is so simple as just picking up the Bible and reading it for themselves, but it is. The word of God transforms our lives by renewing our minds and changing the way we think. When our thoughts change, our actions and our words began to change and match up to God's word. When this happens, get ready, because you are about to receive all that God has promised to give to you through His word.

As a Man Thinketh, so He Is

"As someone thinks within himself, so he is."
(Proverbs 23:7)

Your action and words are often a reflection of what you think about yourself. For example, if you believe that you are not good enough for the job, then you most likely won't be. If you think you can accomplish a great task, you will if God is with you and you are determined. If you think that you cannot do something, you won't, but the question, is what do you say about yourself? If you constantly say, "I cannot do it, I'm just not good enough, this obstacle is too big," then what you think about will be your reality.

Instead of focusing on the negative and all the things that you cannot do, instead focus and think about the positive. Start creating thoughts on how you will finish that new project, how you will overcome that new obstacle, and how you will accomplish all that God has for you to do. When you start doing this, you are taking a step into positioning yourself for victory.

Proverbs 4:23 says, "Be careful how you think, your life is shaped by your thoughts." How do you see yourself? Do you see yourself standing tall and victorious? Or do you see yourself down, defeated, and discouraged? The visual pictures that you see in your mind will translate into actions, which can then affect how you behave and ultimately what comes out of your mouth. So, what should you say?

God wants us to say what He says about us. He says we should say, "I am the righteousness of God in Christ Jesus"

(Romans 10: 6). "I am the head and not the tail, I will lend to many nations and not borrow." [1] "I know that I can do all things through Jesus Christ who strengthens me."[2] "If God is for me, then who can be against me, if God is on my side then whom should I be afraid of?" [3] God wants us to say what He says about us.

What you say about yourself will begin to shape your life, so it is so important to confess things that match God's word over your life. There may have been people in your life who have spoken words of defeat, maybe said you were worthless, good for nothing, or put you down in some way, but you do not have to accept those thoughts. You have the power to control your mind and defeat the lies that the enemy tries so desperately to get you to believe. When the enemy plants thoughts or makes suggestions in your mind, you have the authority to say "NO!"

Perhaps he whispers, "You don't have what it takes, you are not good enough." Or he may cause you to think a thought that you do not agree with. As soon as that wrong or negative thought enters your mind, you must quickly declare in boldness, "I do not accept that thought, that is your thought and statement, not mine. I will not come into agreement with what you say, but will come into agreement with what God says about me!" Our mind is something that we have the power to control, so we must be aware of the enemy's tricks and put a stop to what the enemy tries to do. Paul says, "I discipline my body and keep it under control so that after preaching to others I would not be disqualified." (1 Corinthians 9:27).

It is important to recognize the ploys and devices of the enemy. Satan will use anything or anyone who has a place of significance in your life to discourage you. He may even use your father, mother, friend, or someone important to you to insult you or put negative thoughts into your mind. Parents can be hateful to their children and spouses can criticize you, but the Bible says we do not fight against flesh and blood. You are not fighting your parents, friends, or loved ones who have hurt you. Instead, your fight, according to the word of God, is against the evil rulers and authorities of the unseen world, against mighty powers in this dark world, and evil spirits in the heavenly places (Ephesians 6:12).

If you find yourself in the middle of an argument with a loved one, stop and take a moment to realize that the enemy is using that loved one (to get to you) or come against you to get you unraveled. Instead, fight back with love, which will cause the enemy to squirm and scream in defeat. Don't allow him to deceive you. Your fight is not against man but rather the enemy who is trying to defeat you by using those closest to you.

Changing the way you think changes your perspective, and when you change your perspective and how you view life, you change the way you act and the words you say. It is unbelievable how much power that words can actually have over our

> *Choose to speak words of kindness, gentleness, and love.*

lives. Imagine if you lived every day and spoke words as if they were your last. You most probably would speak with more kindness, gentleness, and love. We should not wait for death to come before we choose to love someone through our words. Jesus showed everyone kindness and love, whether it was the woman at the well, the man at the pool of Bethesda, or his daily conversations with his disciples and others. He used wisdom with every word He spoke and always showed compassion to those that were hurting.

In the same way, if you have been bruised by the words of others and have been hurt in some way, determine in your heart that you will not do the same things that they have done to you. Choose to make a difference in the words that you speak to yourself and the words that you say to those that surround you. I pray, believe, and declare that when you choose to speak as God would speak to both you and others, your life will change in ways that will only increase your love, joy, and peace. When you do this, you will begin take steps towards a better life and one of victory!

CHAPTER 10

Get Rid Of that Old Recording

Many times, we may have a record that plays over and over in our minds. Depending on our childhood, some of these recordings can either be positive or negative. You may have had a record telling you that you are not good enough, you do not have the right skills or talents to accomplish what you have been dreaming about, or you are too old, or don't have the right looks. When you start to hear this, just turn off the recording. You do not have to allow those memories of how people have hurt you, what you have done wrong, or the mistakes you have made play over and over again in your mind. You have the power to shut that recording off.

I have a friend who came from a dysfunctional home where she was fed a great deal of negativity in her life. Although she is a strong Christian now, the enemy used old recordings of negative thoughts to get her down to her lowest point. However, she did not stand and engage and accept the thoughts. Instead, when the enemy tormented her with thoughts, she immediately puts on worship music, sang, or found sermons on YouTube about the issue she was facing and listened until the thoughts fled. She has needed to do this often; however, with each passing day the negative thoughts had less power over her and she was able to stand and fight the enemy with the word of God. Today she is a strong woman of faith that helps to reach many that are hurting in her community.

Are you allowing the enemy to play records of negativity, failure, and lack in your life? If so, you can turn that old recording off and put on a new record. When thoughts come that say, "You have made too many mistakes, you're not good enough," or lies come into your mind, stop and talk back to that voice and say what God says about you. God wants you to say, "I am a new creation in Christ: old things have passed away, behold all things are new!" [1] "I am clean because Jesus made me clean, I belong to Him and He died to set me free from sin and that is why I can stand today."

Speak up and declare, "No weapon formed against me will succeed, and every tongue (including Satan) that rises against me in judgment will fall" (Isaiah 54:17). This is a principle that God wants you and I to stand on. When the enemy attempts to bombard your mind and spirit, fight him off with the word of God and His promises to you. Don't focus on the negative, focus on God's promises and His words to you. You have the power to turn off the old recording. Your mind is not a garbage dump for a pile of negativity. Instead, empty that old smelly trash and start asking God for help to fill your mind with good things.

It is important to take inventory of your thoughts throughout the day. Do your thoughts edify and build you up, or do they bring you down? When the slightest thought of negativity starts to creep in your mind, squash it. Immediately. Put an end to what the enemy is trying to accomplish and the lies he puts in your head (2 Corinthians 2:11, 10:5 KJV). Once the thought has a chance to enter your mind and continue to grow and fester, it can take root within you. However, decide to pull that root out and "reject every kind of evil" or negative thought (1 Thessalonians 5:22). We are not to entertain everything that comes into our minds. Instead, we are to evaluate every thought and see if it lines up with the word of God. If it does not, then stop it right at its onset. (2 Corinthians 10:5)

Start speaking words of hope and victory in your life. Start saying, "I am strong, I am healthy, I have God's favor on me because I am His child." [2] "My sins are forgiven and my record of wrong has been wiped clean, and Jesus loves me and I am adopted into His family." [3] [4] Speaking words of hope and life only encourages us. On the contrary, thinking and speaking words that are opposite to God's word and His truth only hurts us and prevents God's best for our lives. Think about it: if the enemy can get you so wound up in negative thinking, hopelessness, and defeat, he has won and now has the ability to keep you from accomplishing your dreams and God's plan for your life. That is why it is so important to read the word of God for yourself. When the enemy tries to attack you, you can stand up and fight him with God's word [the sword] with which we all fight.

> *Start speaking words of hope and victory in your life*

The only way to turn off that old recording is by turning on a new recording. We should fill our thoughts and minds with good things. Things that bring us hope, joy, and God's peace. For example, when you drive to work, instead of listening to the radio full of music that brings you down, maybe try to listen to a sermon of your favorite preacher, listen to Christian podcasts, audiobooks, or music that builds you up. Listening to sermons or materials in the areas that we are weak can only make us stronger. Try listening to messages on getting rid of negative thinking or "Overcoming doubt and fear." This can only strengthen you in the areas that you are deficient in. If we start putting God's word in us even when we don't need it, we can be sure that it will come out of us when we do need it.

Jeremiah was called to be a prophet to speak to not only the Jews, but to the neighboring nations as a representative of God. However, he felt inadequate and did not feel that he had what it took to accomplish God's plan for his life. Jeremiah felt that he was too young and no one would listen to him and felt he could not speak to the people. Rather, God said to him, "Don't say that you are too young or cannot speak. For you will go to where I send you and speak to whom I tell you to speak to" (Jeremiah 1). The Lord went on to say, "Jeremiah, before I formed you in your mother's womb I knew [and] approved of you [as My chosen instrument]. Before you were born, I separated and set you apart and I appointed you as a prophet to the nations." [5] God had a plan for Jeremiah even before he was born! He knew that Jeremiah may have been strong in certain aspects of his life and weak in others.

However, amid all his inadequacies, God still chose him to accomplish what he had prepared for him to do. Often, we feel that we do not have the talent nor ability to do what God is asking us to do, but the truth is you do! He would not have put the dream or desire in your heart to accomplish what He has called you to do without being there to help you. If God is asking you to preach, then preach. If He has called you to teach, then teach. If He has put a dream in your heart, then pursue it for His glory. God appointed Jeremiah for a special job, as He has also appointed you for special work and assignment, and placed the dreams within you that He has for you. However, if you do not turn off that old recording of negative words within your mind, the enemy can keep you from accomplishing and becoming all that you were meant to be.

Don't Dwell There

Dwelling on our problems gets us nowhere! Dwelling on or worrying about our problems does not change a single thing about what has happened or can happen to us. Situations or troubles may come upon us, but we do not have to let it stop us. The Bible says in Philippians 3:13-14, "But one thing I do is: Forgetting what is behind and straining toward what

> *Philippians 3:13-14, "But one thing I do is: Forgetting what is behind and straining toward what is ahead*

is ahead. I press on toward the goal to win the prize for which God has called me heavenward in Christ Jesus." When you and I are in a race we don't run backward, instead, you aim to run forward. In the same way, don't let your yesterday keep you from accomplishing all that God has in store for you today.

God does not want you to focus on the past and everything that went wrong. When we do this, we stay so focused on the negative and on our problems that we forget to live and enjoy our lives right here, right now. When new believers come to Christ for the first time, they often struggle with their past mistakes. However, God has said that he has washed and cleansed us free from our sins (Psalms 51:2). When we come into the family of God, he makes us a new creation in Christ, old things are passed away, and behold all things become new (2 Corinthians 5:17).

God died on the cross so that you and I can be saved from destruction. When you accept Him into your heart, you allow the Holy Spirit to come in and do work that only God can do. I love what the Bible says in Isaiah 1:18. God speaks to us and says, "Though your sins are like scarlet, they shall be as white as snow; though they are red like crimson, they shall be like wool." That means we have a clean slate before God and have the opportunity to repent and ask forgiveness for the past mistakes we have made. Jesus died on the cross for both you and me because He loves us and wants good things for us. Don't focus on all the things that have brought you down in the past because God says, "This is the day that the Lord has made, so I will rejoice and be glad in it"! (Psalms 118:24)!

When people in your past have hurt you, whether in small or big ways, it can be painful. Often no one will understand the magnitude of the hurt that you may have gone through, nor have seen those tears, pain, or sleepless nights that you may have endured, but God does! He has promised to help vindicate you and deal with the matter Himself. God does not want us to take revenge into our own hands. Instead, He wants us to trust Him and let Him fight our battles. To move forward and forget the hurts in the past, God wants us to forgive those who have hurt us.

You may think, "Oh, God, here we go, do we have to talk about forgiveness again?" However, forgiveness is key! Forgiving those who have hurt you helps to remove the chains that have been holding you down and opens the door to a pathway of freedom. Forgiveness is not always easy and may take some time. However, it is important to work through those feelings to receive the victory. If freedom from past hurts is what you're looking for, then God can help you.

I heard a story of a young woman that grew up in a very negative environment. She told me that her parents would fight all the time, curse at each other, and take it out on her and her siblings. This woman's father would criticize her for minor mistakes and called her horrible names. He told her she was worthless and would not amount to anything in life. Her parents provided for her basic needs but criticized her for everything. They came from a broken home and were mistreated and abused. She dreamed of the day that she could leave home and start a new life, a life away from her parents. The day came that she was able to leave home, and she thought she would not have to deal with the pain again.

However, she was wrong and the pain followed her daily. She would often replay those negative thoughts and rehashed the memories over and over again until that it would consume her. She would visit her parents occasionally. They seemed to have forgotten what they had done, but she did not. For years she dwelled on those thoughts and hated them, but the hatred kept her in bondage. She realized that she was the only one suffering and carrying the burden day in and day out.

Until one day she decided to forgive them, just as God had forgiven her. She realized that God requires that we forgive each other just as He forgave her of her many sins. Often, we want people to forgive our mistakes and offenses quickly, but we do not want to forgive them. This woman decided to forgive her parents of their shortcomings just as God had forgiven her. She wanted to be free of the bondage and chains that the enemy wanted to keep her in.

It is God's will for us to forgive those that have hurt us because He knows it will set us free. He loves us and has commanded us to forgive each other, to the point that He specifically outlined this in the "Lord's Prayer." God would not have added this to our "daily" prayer unless he felt it was of great importance. When we start to recite and speak the Lord's Prayer over our lives, we begin to know the heart of God. Speaking the word of God and the Lord's Prayer daily only helps us grow in understanding His heart more.

The Importance of Forgiveness

Esau was asked by his father Isaac to catch some game and make him his favorite soup so that he could bless him. Isaac was getting old and blind and wanted to give his eldest son his birthright, which is a privileged blessing for being the oldest. However, Jacob, his younger brother, with the help of his mother, went to great lengths to dress like Esau by putting on his clothes and wearing goatskin to emulate Esau's hairy appearance.

Now Jacob, pretending to be Esau, gave the soup to his father to get his brother's birthright instead. When Esau came home after hunting the game, he also prepared the soup to present to his father Isaac just like his father had asked him to do. When Isaac, who was blind, realized that he had been fooled he began to tremble and told Esau that his younger brother Jacob had stolen his blessing.

Esau began to beg his father for another blessing but his father said that the anointed blessing was already given away. Esau broke down and yelled and cried to his father and said, "Please just give me another blessing. Don't you have another blessing you can give me?" However, Isaac, still trembling, said to his son, "I cannot, your brother has taken away your birthright." Esau then cried out and said, "No wonder his name is Jacob, for now he has cheated me twice. First, he took my birthright as the firstborn, and now he has stolen my blessing." Esau became angry and wanted to kill his brother. Knowing this, Jacob fled to Haran in fear and for safety. (Genesis 27)

Later in the story, we find that God did vindicate Esau. Jacob himself was deceived and spent 14 years working for a relative that also deceived him on several occasions. Many years later through their victories and failures, both learned to forgive each other with God's help. Jacob, after many years apart from his brother, asked Esau for his forgiveness. When they finally met, Jacob bowed down before Esau in a position of humbleness and asked for his brother's mercy. Esau lovingly forgave him. They hugged and cried and began to have the brotherly relationship they were always meant to have.

It is not God's will for us to be filled with, resentment, anger, bitterness, and unforgiveness. Even if those who have hurt us never apologize for their mistakes, God wants us to be the bigger person and forgive them anyway. Isaiah 43:18-19 says, "Forget the former things and do not dwell on the past. See, I am doing a new thing! Now it springs up; do you not perceive it? God wants to do a new thing in you!" When you choose to forgive the person

> Isaiah 43:18-19 says, "Forget the former things and do not dwell on the past.

that has hurt you, you allow God to set you free. God is ready to do a new work in both you and me. He wants to give us a new beginning, a fresh new outlook on life, and open doors for new opportunities.

However, we must be willing to let go of our past and be open to all that God has for us. If someone has hurt you today, pray for them, speak words of blessing over them, and ask God to lead them into knowing Him more. If you have hurt others, ask them for forgiveness and make amends. God will help you as you begin to take one step forward on the path of love, freedom, and victory!

The Confessions of Your Mouth

Confessions are important! The most important confession that you and I can make is to acknowledge and confess with our lips that Jesus is Lord and believe in our hearts that God raised Him from the dead. The Bible says that if you do this, then you will be saved. When we acknowledge, speak openly, and confess with our mouths that Jesus is Lord, we recognize His power, authority, and majesty as God. We believe in our hearts that Jesus Christ died on the cross for our sins. In doing this we are made right in His sight, freed of the guilt of sin and made acceptable to God. This confirms our salvation, and the scriptures say, "Whoever believes in Him, [trusts and relies on Him] will never be put to shame or be disappointed" (Romans 10:8-11, AMP).

This is the most important confession that we can make. Beside this, there is no other. When we become saved, God's spirit begins to work and operate in and through us. We become a Child of God, receive His grace, and are adopted into His family. (Galatians 4:5, John 1:12, Ephesians 2:8). Jesus will receive you with open arms and the Bible says that "all of heaven and the angels rejoice when one sinner repents and comes into a relationship with Christ" (Luke 15:7). This is exciting news! That means that God has given you and I a means by which we can have a relationship with Him and be in His presence forever.

When you have a personal relationship with Christ you become a new creation in Christ. The old things pass away and God begins to do a new work within you that will bring you life and hope. If you would like to accept Him into your heart today then I can help lead you into the prayer of salvation. You can say, "Lord Jesus, I ask that You come into my heart today and forgive me of my sins. I know that I am a sinner and I have made many mistakes, but I ask that You wash me and make me clean. I confess that You are my Lord and Savior and I believe in my heart that You died and rose again on the third day, so that I may have life and live for all eternity with You. I love You, praise You, and I want to thank You for all that you have done for me and will do for me in my future. Thank You, Lord Jesus."

If you just asked Jesus to come into your heart today the Bible says, "All of heaven and the angels are rejoicing," and frankly... so am I! Congratulations, if you have asked Jesus Christ to be your savior. I encourage you to find a local Bible-based church to help you in your growth and your new walk with the Lord. I know that you will be so glad that you did!

Confessing Our Sins Together

As a new believer, or at any point in our Christian life, it is important for us to first confess our sins to God and each other. Confessing our sins to God means we become real with God. It means that we take off the phony mask that we often hide behind, and become open and honest before God. God already knows who we are on the inside, our past mistakes, where we have gone and what we have done, but the good news is, He loves us anyway! 1 John 1:9 says that "if we confess our sins, He is faithful and just to forgive us of our sins and to cleanse us from all unrighteousness."

God is very willing and wants to forgive you, but you have to take that first step and come to Him in humbleness, knowing that He is awesome, creator of the universe and the King of Kings. He died so that you and I could have life, which most importantly leads to eternal life. That is why it is so important to share your heart with Him. It is okay to talk to God from your heart and say, "God, I have messed up, I have made so many mistakes and I have no idea what to do or where to go." Or it is okay to say, "God, I don't want to live like this, I need You to help me and change me."

Let me tell you today, God is waiting with His arms open wide to help you through your pain, your past, and all your troubles. He wants to be a part of your everyday life,

He wants to bless and provide for you. He wants to bless you abundantly and give you the desires of your heart, but we must first come to Him with an open heart. When you do this God's light and His peace will fill your heart and mind!

One way that we can start this is to sit at His feet, which means in a place or position of humbleness. You can start on your knees or however you feel most comfortable and talk to Him as your loving heavenly Father. Come to Him like you're a child running into your daddy's arms. Cry out to Him and tell Him everything that is on your heart, almost like you are getting rid of all the junk that has been on your chest. Share your anxieties, worries, fears, and failures. Share your love for Him, your desires, your hopes and dreams for the future.

Ask Him to talk to you as well, then stop and listen for some time. When you do this, you will begin to feel God's presence and His loving arms around you. God's Holy Spirit, who is our comforter and advocate, will come into your heart to help and strengthen you, and draw you close to God's heart. (John 14:26; John 15:26, Ephesians 3:16). When we confess our sins to God, it cleanses us and changes us from within.

When I was a child, I would come home, run to my room, and run next to the window. I would look up at heaven and talk to God. I would tell Him all about my day, share my girly secrets, tell Him all my corny jokes and talk to Him as if he was my best friend because He truly was and is! He was someone that I could talk to without judgment or scorn. He loved me and was just as excited to spend time with me as I was with Him.

I could feel His presence fill my room and fill my heart with joy. God wants to have an intimate relationship with you as well. He wants to be your closest friend, your heavenly Father, and your first love. The Bible says, "seek ye first the kingdom of God, and all these things shall be added unto you." (Matthew 6:33). Will you let Him into your heart today, to change you and make you whole? If so, He is ready and waiting for you, with His arms open wide. Spend time talking to God about your heart, your feelings, and even your day. God wants to spend time and talk with you as well. When you do this, your relationship with the Lord will go to a higher level.

Speak God's Word over Your Life

Speaking God's word over your life is so important! God's word empowers us, strengthens us, and causes us to stand in victory. When we start to declare what God says about us, we start forming our new identity in Him. Sometimes it is hard to know where to start or what to do, especially

> *Start making these declarations over your life every day or until it sinks into your heart*

when you have not had a good start in life. You may have had a complicated family history or other reasons that make it difficult for you to know who you are in Christ. When we start to confess God's word over our lives, it puts a seal on who we are, and God's spirit comes alive in us. You can start by making a list of what God says about you and who He has created you to be.

Start making these declarations over your life every day or until it sinks into your heart, then the enemy cannot convince you otherwise. You may have to repeat these declarations over and over again, but when you do this, you start taking on God's identity for you and will begin to walk in victory.

Start by saying:

1. I am a new person in Christ, my old life is gone, and I belong to Christ (See 2 Corinthians 5:17).

2. I am a child of God because I believe in Him. God has adopted me into His family (James 1:12, Ephesians 1:5).

3. I have been chosen by God, I am a royal priesthood, and I will proclaim God's goodness because He pulled me out of darkness into His marvelous light (1 Peter 2:9).

4. I have been chosen before the foundations of the world. I am holy and without blame before God (Ephesians 1:4; 1 Peter 1:16).

5. God has great plans for me. Plans to give me a hope and a future (Jeremiah 29:11).

6. I am born of God and the evil one cannot touch me (1 John 5:18, 1 John 4:4).

7. I am no longer condemned because God has forgiven me from the law of sin and death (Romans 8:1-2).

8. God died on the cross for me, and because of His wounds I have been healed (1 Peter 2:24).

9. God knew me before I was born, I am fearfully and wonderfully made (Psalms 139: 13-14).

10. I am more than a conqueror through Jesus Christ who loves me (Romans 8:37).

11. Jesus has set me free and I am free indeed (John 8:36).

12. I will be strong in the Lord and the power of His might (Ephesians 6:10).

Speaking God's word over your life fills you with power and the ability to walk in His strength and truth. Every day as you apply and speak God's word over your life it will begin to sink into your spirit, strengthen you, and give you the power to withhold the darts from the enemy that he tries to bring against you. Satan will try to penetrate your mind with lies about your past mistakes and failures, but when you start to say what God says about you, the enemy will begin to lose his grip over you, and you will surely stand in victory.

Make Declarations Over Your Life

There is power in stating who you are. When we declare who we are and what we would like to be, those words take root deep within our souls and will start to come alive in us. You can start by making a list of what you want to see change and declaring it in advance. For example, the Bible says, "Let the weak say I am strong" (Joel 3:10) God did not say, "Wait until you feel strong to say that you are strong." No, He said, "Even amid your weakness, declare that you are strong!"

With each declaration your heart beats stronger, your bones begin to strengthen, your ears begin to listen, and every fiber of your being begins to recognize the words of God that you declare over your life. As you begin to declare God's word over your situation in faith, your body must come in alignment with God's word. Hebrews 4:12 says, "For the word of God is alive and powerful. It is sharper than the sharpest two-edged sword, cutting between soul and spirit, between joint and marrow." That means that when you speak the words that God has spoken over your life, those words go down deep. It seeps into your spirit and soul and between the crevices of your joints and marrow. When this happens, your body must stand at attention and heed the authority of the word of God.

No matter what you are going through, begin to speak over your situation and say, "I will live and not die, but declare the works of the Lord" (Psalms 118:17). Despite what the situation looks like, speak in faith, even if you do not see the results. That is what faith is all about. Faith is believing before you can see it. Hebrews 11:1 says, "Now faith is the substance of things hoped for, the evidence of things not seen." Without hope, we are not able to have faith, and without faith it is impossible to please God (Hebrews 11:6). That is what God wants to see from us. He wants to see our faith in action. Mark 11:24 says, "Therefore I tell you, whatever you ask for in prayer, believe that you have received it, and it will be yours."

> *Faith is the substance of things hoped for, the evidence of things not seen (Hebrews 11:1)*

If you find yourself struggling financially, pray and start declaring, "I am coming out of debt, I am the head and not the tail, I will lend to many nations and not borrow." If you want to be successful, start declaring, "I will prosper and succeed in all that I touch" (Deuteronomy 30:9). If you feel weak, start saying, "I am brave, I am strong in Jesus' name" (Joshua 1:9). It is not enough to wish upon a star, but instead, you need to put your faith in action. If there are areas in your life that you want to see change, start declaring that change in advance.

Before you leave your house, start speaking blessings over your life that are in agreement with God's word. When you do this, God's supernatural power goes to work for you. The more you declare God's word and His promises out loud, the more His word will take root in your spirit, causing your faith to rise. Even though you may not be able to see it right now, the more you continue to declare God's promises and say what God says about you, you will have it!

If you are struggling in an area start declaring:

1. "I am strong" (Ephesians 6:10).

2. "I am brave" (Joshua 1:9).

3. "I am healed in Jesus' name" (Psalms 118:17).

4. If you need healing or want to live a long life say, "I will live and not die, but declare the works of the Lord" (Psalms 118:17). Or, "God, you are restoring health unto me and have healed me of my wounds" (Jeremiah 30:17).

5. "I will be green and vital, producing fruit into old age" (Psalms 92:14).

6. "I am coming out of debt - the Lord is my shepherd and I will lack not one thing" (Psalms 23:1).

7. Women, you can declare in your marriage, "My husband loves me as much as his flesh. He loves, nourishes, and cherishes me just like Christ does for the church" (Ephesians 5:25-29).

8. Husbands can declare, "I am tenderhearted with my wife, and only dwell on what is excellent and the wonderful things about her" (Ephesians 4:32, Philippians 4:8).

9. If you feel faint and weary, repeat "I can do all things through Christ who strengthens me, through the power of Jesus Christ" (Philippians 4:13).

10. If you want to see a change in your children start declaring, "My children obey and honor their parents" (Ephesians 6:1,2). "They respect their teachers and all in authority" (Romans 13:1,2).

Start speaking in the direction that you are seeking. Declaring what you want to see changed in advance puts you in a position to receive all that God has in store for you. Continue to repeat your declarations until it becomes rooted in your spirit and you feel your faith rise. Don't focus on all the negatives and everything that might not work, instead put your faith into action. Start speaking blessings, God's favor, and his power over your life and your family. When you begin to do this, you will begin to see a change not only in yourself, but in the lives of those around you. God loves you very much and He wants you to declare your victory in advance. Trust Him to help you and He promised that He will.

CHAPTER **11**

Your Faith is Vital to See Results

Speaking faith into your life is vital to seeing God move in your situation and for Him to do the miraculous. Without faith, it is impossible to please God and it prohibits us from reaching our highest potential. There is great power in speaking words of faith over your situation and in alignment with God's word. God wants us to come into agreement with what He says is possible. Mark 11:22-24 (AMP) says that Jesus replied to the disciples, "Have faith in God [constantly]. I assure you and most solemnly say to you, whoever says to this mountain, be lifted up and thrown into the sea, and does not doubt in his heart [in God's unlimited power], but believes that what he says is going to take place, it will be done for him [in accordance with God's word]."

God is saying your words have the power to change things. Use your words to change the atmosphere and call forth those things of which are not, as though they were (Romans 4:17). The Bible says, "let the weak say that I am strong" (Joel 3:10). That means God wants you to say things in advance even if you cannot see it. If you are having trouble paying off your bills, begin to say, "I am coming out of debt, even if it takes me one step at a time, I am going to get these bills paid down." Start by declaring your victory even before you begin to see it.

Or, "I am going to lose those 15 lbs.," and make a plan on how to do this. The more you speak forth what you desire, the closer you are to achieving it. The opposite of this is true as well.

Let's say, for example, it's flu season and they are giving out flu shots at work. While standing in line your friend begins to say, "I'm probably going to get the flu, I do every year, it's like I have a big red dot on my forehead that says

> *Our body, mind, soul, and spirit are connected.*

pick me, and sure enough, I get it. I am always sick during the flu season." Do you think this person has a chance of getting the flu? The likelihood that she is going to get the flu is high because she is calling it in with her words.

The Bible says, in Proverbs 6:2, that "we are ensnared by the words of our mouth" We can set a trap for ourselves by speaking words of defeat and misfortune. Every time you say things that you don't mean, unconsciously you start to believe them. The more we start saying something negative over and over again, the more it gets ingrained in our spirit over time. Our body, mind, soul, and spirit are connected, so whatever we say can have tremendous power to impact us physically and mentally. It is important to know that God is a God of faith. In all aspects of the Bible, He calls us to have faith.

We can call forth God's blessings, His favor, anointing, health and healing, and our joy by coming into agreement with God's word and speaking His promises over our lives. Begin to pray and speak out your end desired result. 1 John 5:14-15 says, "This is the confidence we have in approaching God: that if we ask anything according to His will, He hears us, and if we know that He hears us then we know that we will have whatever we ask of Him." The more you call forth your desire in faith, the more likely you are to receiving the answer to your prayer.

For example, if you are believing for a new paid-off house, you can pray and say "Lord, I pray and ask You for a home that is Your best for me. I want to be debt-free and I ask for a debt-free home in Jesus' name. I receive it by faith and I want to thank You for the answer." Now begin to start thanking God for answering your prayer. Get happy and keep on thanking God until your faith begins to rise. Once you pray in faith, you then need to have the corresponding action to that faith to be able to get the results you desire.

God wants you to seek His face and, and have expectancy while you wait for His answer. He says, "Call unto me and I will answer you, and I will show you great and mighty things of which you do not know." (Jeremiah 33:3). We need faith to be able to please God to see our miracle. Speaking the end desired result of what you need by faith puts you in a position to receive all that God has in store for us.

It is important for you to prayerfully take some time to examine your words and to evaluate if you are speaking faith into your situation or not. Are you speaking what God has said about You in his word, or are you speaking words that the enemy can use against you? Decide today to speak words that build your faith and not words that will tear you down. God wants to do the impossible for you, but it begins with faith. You have the power, with God's help, to accomplish everything He has placed in your heart and I believe that you can get there!

God Can Do the Impossible

Faith is the element that is needed for God to do anything in your life. The Bible says that faith pleases God and without it, it is impossible to please Him (Hebrews 11:6). When you put your faith in God it means that you know He exists, and if you know He

> Faith is the element that is needed for God to do anything in your life.

exists then you will know that His words are true and you can trust and believe in Him (1 John 5:15).

Your faith has the supernatural power to believe God for the impossible. Even amid uncertainties, when you just don't know what else to do, having faith in God is what will open the doors for God to do the work you are asking Him to do. Jesus said all things are possible to him that believes (Mark 9:23). When you believe, God's power is released from heaven and can go to work for you.

It was Job's faith and trust in God in the good times and bad times that caused him to be blessed and to receive double. Job had every reason to throw in the towel and doubt God when he lost his home, his possessions, and his children all at one time. This must have been gut-wrenching for him, and yet even amid his suffering, his faith and trust in God stood strong. Job cried out to God and shared his heart with God, and God heard his cry.

Noah was a man that trusted and obeyed God despite looking like a fool amongst the people of the land. God told Noah to build an ark and warned him that the people of the land were very wicked and about to be destroyed. Noah began to build an ark out of trust and obedience to God. He believed God's word and was faithful to do what God had called him to do. The people of the land mocked, spit, and called Noah crazy, but because of his faith, Noah continued to work diligently at building the ark and ultimately saw God's words come true (See Genesis 6-7).

It was through faith that three Jewish boys named Shadrach, Meshach, and Abednego refused to bow down to King Nebuchadnezzar. Even though King Nebuchadnezzar made a command throughout his nation that everyone must bow down and worship his golden image, they stood strong in their faith. The King commanded that anyone who disobeyed his law would be thrown into the fiery furnace to die.

However, despite the threats, the boys stood their ground and did not waver. Shadrach, Meshach, and Abednego told King Nebuchadnezzar that they did not need to defend themselves before him, but that God would deliver them from his hands. These three boys spoke up and defended their belief in God. The King was outraged and threw them into the fiery furnace, yet God was in the midst of them. When the King looked into the fire, he did not just see three boys in the fire, rather he saw a fourth and His name was Jesus! (see Daniel 3)

In the same way, God can rescue you. He can do the miraculous if you believe. If you are sick, He can heal you. If you are in financial ruin or do not have the money to pay for your needs, He can bring you out and supply all your needs. If your family is falling apart, He can restore you and bring you back together. God can do the impossible if you put your trust in Him and believe for the miraculous. I encourage you to talk to God from your heart. Tell Him how much you love Him, about your needs, and thank Him for his answers. Psalms 34:17 says, "the righteous cry out, and the LORD hears them; He delivers them from all their troubles."

God sees your tears. His eyes are upon you and His ears are attentive to your prayers (1 Peter 3:12). When we pray God has already supplied the answer. It is God's will for you to be healed, to have financial prosperity, be debt-free, and live in abundance. Jesus died that we could have life in Him. A life that has purpose, is meaningful, joyful, and eternal. Keep your eyes on Him and trust God to work amidst your impossible situation and watch as He moves on your behalf.

In the Midst of Uncertainties

In my life, I have always come to God with child-like faith and God has done miraculous things for me as a result. Growing up, my parents were not extremely well off, but God had always provided for our needs. At the age of 18, I was getting ready to go off to college and I was not sure how I was going to pay for my tuition and books. My parents did not have the means to pay tuition for my siblings and me. So, I took out some loans but hesitated to take out too much, because I did not want to be in debt.

One day, I heard a few kids at school talking about scholarships that could help pay for college tuition fees and I thought, "Maybe I can do this!" God was good. I prayed every day that God would make a way for me to get the money that I needed and I tried my very best. There were some scholarships that required essays to be written before you could even be considered. I wrote a few short essays to apply for scholarships online but I never ended up getting anything for them. I also heard about a few scholarships that were going to be made available at the school, so I thought I would try. During my high school years, I was a part of an Anchor Club, which is an International Youth Service organization, along with many of the other girls in my class. The Anchor Club was offering a one-time $500 scholarship to an individual who they felt best answered a series of questions that they had for each student.

When it was time to get interviewed by the board members of the club, each of us girls went one by one into the private room filled with many of the board members to present ourselves. Each girl went in and got interviewed and I felt as if I had no chance to win in comparison to them. They were popular, their mothers were involved in so many organizations and clubs within the school, and they seemed as if they had everything going for them. Their sense of pride, excitement, and confidence left me feeling like I would have a low chance of winning.

> *Do your best and God will do the rest*

Nonetheless, I thought to myself, "I am going to try my best and just be myself." It felt as if the line took forever, and I was the second person from the last to go in. I was nervous but would repeatedly say under my breath, "I am going to give it my best and let God do the rest. God, I may not be like the others, but I know I can do all things with your strength. Please lead me through" (Philippians 4:13).

I went into that meeting, believing and putting my trust in God's hands, and gave it my best shot. I remember leaving that interview unsure if I did a good job. The girls that were also competing with me were all giddy with joy, smiling and saying to each other, "No, I think you did a great job, you probably got it! No, for sure, Carrie, you probably got it, your mom was one of the judges." On and on they went deciding who amongst them were the winners.

An hour went by and all the girls waited anxiously outside of the office door to hear what the board members had decided. I was unsure because it appeared unlikely out of all the girls lined up outside that I would be chosen or even considered. The door opened and the president of the board pulled out a sheet of paper, and silence filled the room. She said, "We have had a wonderful time interviewing all the candidates here and you have all done a great job. However, we feel the candidate that we have chosen exemplified the characteristics that best represent our club. She has shown integrity, leadership, and academic skills, helped with community services, and is someone that we feel is the right choice for us. The winner of this scholarship is Julie Kurian!" The room fell silent and I was shocked! I'm sure, looking back now, my mouth was probably wide open! LOL. I had no words to say, I just remembered all the empty stares of the girls around me, looking at me as if asking, "Why her?"

I slowly but gratefully stepped forward and received the certificate as they congratulated me. The truth is, I knew that I did not say anything outstanding that day, but one thing I did know was that God was with me and He gave me the words to say that day. Just like Moses, who did not feel he was eloquent with speech or good with words, yet God told him, "I am the one who has made your mouth and I will fill it with the right words to say" (See Exodus 4:10-12).

In the same way, I prayed, and I took a step of faith to be able to help pay for my tuition, and God made a way for me before those judges. I am often reminded of His faithfulness to me in big and even small things. God is faithful and able to do the impossible as we put our faith and trust in Him (see Matthew 19:26, Mark 10:27). He can do the same for you! Trust him with impossibilities in your life, and as you pray and seek Him, wait expectantly for the answer.

Pray, Ask, and Activate your Faith

Faith requires that we do something instead of sitting around and wishing upon a star. We need to put action behind our faith and let God do the rest. It is not beneficial to ask God to help us pass a test in school if we do not take the time to study. Often, we want God to take the first step in helping us; however, God requires us to take the first step to help ourselves. He wants us to try to do things to the best of our abilities and He will do what we cannot do. If you pray that God would help you lose weight, then it is important to take the first step by creating a plan to help get there.

If you ask God to help you get out of debt, then it requires that you sit down and look at how you are spending your money. It is important to take responsibility and make the necessary changes to get you where you want to be. We need to put action behind our faith. When God sees this, He is moved to give us the answer.

There was a woman in the Bible who suffered from a bleeding disorder for 12 years. She had put her faith into action by going to her physicians first for treatment and doing all that she could do in the natural world. In other words, she tried her best to get healed with all the options that she had available at that time. However, despite her attempts, she only began to grow worse over time.

I can imagine that she may have been discouraged, hurt, and feeling alone in her illness. She may have even felt like giving up; however, the Bible says that she never gave up. She began to try everything and anything possible to find a cure. She used all the resources that were around her to be able to help herself and do what she could do in the natural world. Despite her attempts, she knew that only God could heal her and she was determined to get it.

During her search, she *heard* about a man named Jesus who was coming through her town. She was so desperate that she was willing to do anything. She had already done everything she could do in the natural world, but now she needed the Son of Man to do the supernatural. Culturally, it was taboo for a woman that was menstruating or losing blood to come out of her home, and especially to go as far as attempting to touch Jesus. Nonetheless, she was determined and would have rather risked her life and taken a chance than to stay within the boundaries of her home and die. She was in bondage and wanted deliverance.

When she attempted to get to Jesus, she encountered an obstacle that seemed impossible to get through. There was a mob of people trying to get to Jesus at the same time she was. They were pushing and shoving and pulling at Him, yet despite it all, this woman was relentless. She said to herself repeatedly, "If only I can touch the hem of His garment, I know I can be healed. If only I can touch the hem of His garment, I know I can be healed. If only I can touch the hem of His garment I will be healed" (See Mark 5)

Her words grew more determined and louder as she got closer to Jesus. She spoke out and encouraged herself by repeating what she wanted to happen. She activated her faith by moving forward not only through the words of her mouth but through her actions. She needed a miracle and was desperate to get it. I can even imagine that she may have crawled to get through the mob to touch the hem of Jesus's garment.

She persistently spoke words of faith, despite her hopeless situation, rather than caving in and speaking words of doubt and hopelessness. Finally, she was able to reach Jesus, and she came behind him and touched the back of his cloak. Immediately her bleeding stopped, and she was freed from the burden of her incurable disease. This woman is a prime example of putting faith into action. She reached out to Jesus to be able to touch Him so that He would make her whole.

Often, we wait on God to make the first move and to open doors for us; however, He asks for us to take the first step. Faith without works is dead, and faith alone is not enough. Unless you activate your faith by acting on what you believe, then it does not bring you any answers. When you spend time in prayer ask God for what you need. The Bible says, "You have not because you ask not." When you ask, believe God, believe His words to you, and God says when you do this, you will have what you ask for. (James 4:2-3, Matthew 21:22)

Expect Your Miracle

Once you pray and have taken action on what God has put in your heart, and have come in agreement with your mouth, the next step is to have a spirit of expectation. Expect your miracle. If we ask God for a miracle, then we need to act as if we have already received it. The worse thing that we can do is pray for something and not believe it will happen.

When we expect miracles, we are keeping a lookout. We are looking for the answers expectantly and believing that God is faithful and able to do the impossible (Luke 1:37 NIV). "Therefore, I tell you, whatever you ask for in prayer, believe that you have received it, and it will be yours" (Mark 11:24; Matthew 21:22). Jesus wants us to believe in advance that we have already received our miracle.

God has given you the ability to speak, and He wants you to pray and ask for your needs while believing that you have already received the answer in advance. He does not want you to be anxious or worried about anything. Instead, we are to pray about everything, and thank Him for the answers (Philippians 4:6-7). It is not God's plan for you to be overwhelmed and dwelling on all your problems. Instead, He wants us to think about whatever is true, whatever is noble, whatever is right, pure, lovely, admirable, excellent, and worthy of praise! (Philippians 4: 6-8). Centering your minds on good things allows you to have a joyful spirit while you are waiting for your answer.

> *Centering your minds on good things allows you to have a joyful spirit while you are waiting for your answer.*

Have you ever prayed for something persistently and eventually reached your answer? Or, have there been times in your life that you have asked God for what you need, yet you don't see anything happening? In those times the Bible encourages us not to lose heart, nor give up, but to continue to pray persistently until we receive the answer. Matthew 7: 7-8 says, "Keep on asking, and you will be given what you ask for. Keep on looking, and you will find. Keep on knocking, and the door will be opened to you." Jesus makes it pretty clear here that He does not want us to give up when we don't see the answer, even when things seem impossible.

There have been many times in my life that I have needed an answer from the Lord. I took the time to fast and pray and set my mind toward God. I was determined and cried out to Him for the answer until He gave me His answer. When I did this, God was faithful to answer my prayers. Your humble persistence shows God that you mean business and shows Him that you are serious and need an answer to your cry. An example of this is shown in the Bible of the persistent widow and an unjust judge.

> *Keep asking, seeking and knocking and the door will be opened to you.*

There was a judge in a certain city who did not fear God nor care about man. A widow of that city came to him repeatedly, saying, "Give me justice in this dispute with my enemy." She asked him constantly, day in and day out. The judge ignored her for a while, but finally, he said to himself, "I don't fear God nor care about man, but this woman is driving me crazy! I'm going to see that she gets justice because she is wearing me out with her *constant requests!*" Jesus said if this unjust judge was able to give this woman justice in the end, would not God also do the same for His people who cry out to Him day and night? (Luke 18:6) "Will He keep putting them off? I tell you; he will grant justice to them quickly!" (See Luke 18:1-8) God loves us and is very happy to give us good gifts. He wants us to keep asking, seeking, and knocking until the door opens for us to receive the answer to our prayers. (Matthew 7:7-8). Call out to Him, pray, seek His face, and expect your miracle!

Go Tell it on the Mountain

When you and I got saved and accepted Jesus Christ as our savior, we asked God to come into our hearts so that we can become a new person in Christ. To know Jesus Christ as our personal savior is the greatest gift that anyone can ever have! Allowing Christ to come into your hearts allows God to cleanse us of our sins, and make us right with Him so that we can have eternal life with Him in heaven (1 John 1:7-9). Once we have received this great gift, God commands us to tell others about Him throughout the world.

He says, "Therefore go and make disciples of all nations, baptizing them in the name of the Father, Son, and Holy Spirit, teaching them to obey everything I have commanded you" (See Matthew 28:19-20). God wants to save the whole world from death and destruction and that is why He requires us to tell others about Him. The Bible says that all the people in the world belong to Him. He loves every one of us no matter what nation, language, or tribe we come from. It is not His will that any of us would perish but have everlasting life (John 3:16, 2 Peter 3:9). This salvation allows us to be with Him in heaven, rejoicing and celebrating for His lovingkindness and goodness towards us.

Often, we may feel inadequate or not capable of witnessing to others; however, God is not asking for perfection. He is asking that we be available and obedient by telling others about him. Jesus said in Acts 1:8 that "we will receive the power from the Holy Spirit to be able to witness and tell others about Him. He wants us to go and preach the gospel into all the world, and to the ends of the earth (Mark 16:15-16).

If God has done anything for you, decide to declare His praises and tell others about the wonderful things He has done for you. Let your light shine for God by showing love to others, helping them, and praying for their needs that they would glorify God because of you (Matthew 5:16) Don't be ashamed of what people may think of you, but instead be bold, and prayerfully take a step of faith by sharing God's word and His love with those around you (Romans 1:16). If you are afraid to verbally speak to someone about Jesus, then it is perfectly fine to pass out Bible tracts, slip a note to someone, write emails, text, or use social media to spread the news.

Scripture tells us that the Gospel of Jesus Christ will be proclaimed throughout the whole world as a testimony to all nations before the end will come (see Matthew 24:14). God is the one who has made your mouth, and He will give you the ability to speak with the help of the Holy Spirit. [1] Matthew 5:15-16 says, "You are the light of [Christ to] the world. A city set on a hill cannot be hidden. Nor does *anyone* light a lamp and put it under a basket, but on a lampstand, and it gives light to all who are in the house."

Let your light shine before men in such a way that they may see your good deeds *and* moral excellence, and [recognize and honor and] glorify your Father who is in heaven. When you take the time to tell others about Christ, the lives of many around you will be changed forever. Let's take time to share God's love to those in need, and God's presence will be with us as we do.

CHAPTER 12

Speak Words that Heal

Words are a beautiful thing when they are used in the right way. They can build up, edify, encourage, and give confidence to those that hear them. The right word spoken at the right time can be life changing. Have you ever met a person in the hospital that was dealing with an illness or a life-threatening condition? The last thing that they need from someone visiting them in the hospital is a word that brings them down. People naturally do not respond well to discouragement or words that pull them down or make them feel worse.

The right word spoken at the right time can be life changing (See Proverbs 15:23). The saying is true that if you have nothing good to say, then it is best not to say anything at all. When we speak words of hope to those hurting, we lift their spirits during the difficult times and can breathe faith and life into their situation. Words of life and hope bring joy, peace, comfort, and a smile to those who are hurting and in need of our love, encouragement, and support. God can use you to be that source of comfort if you are willing.

For example, if you know of a loved one who is battling a difficult situation, whether it be a discouraging illness, a proceeding court case, or a difficult marriage, you can make a difference by sharing a Bible verse that perhaps says, "Do not fear, for I am with you; do not be dismayed, for I am your God. I will strengthen you and help you; I will uphold you with my righteous right hand" [1] Or says, "When you go through deep waters, I will be with you. When you go through rivers of difficulty, you will not drown. When you walk through the fire of oppression, you will not be burned up and the flames will not consume you" (Isaiah 41:10).

These are some verses that have encouraged me during the most difficult times of my life. God says to us, "Let your words be gentle, soothing, and comforting to the one that hears it" (Proverbs 15:1, Proverbs 16:24). Your words make a difference to those who surround you! God does not want us to be bogged down with depression and discouragement. He wants us to be light-hearted and free, to come to Him with all of our worries and troubles, and lay them at His feet. You have the great privilege to point those that are hurting to the one that can heal, that can help, and the one that has the power to change things.

When we use our words to heal a person that is discouraged or broken-hearted, we bring a smile to their faces, lift their spirits, and give them hope. The Bible says, "Using pleasant and (kind) words are like a honeycomb, it brings sweetness to the soul, and comfort and healing to the body" (Proverbs 16:24). When others smile because of your kind words it will also bring a smile to your face and increase your joy. Even though we may go through tough situations of our own, trusting God and keeping a joyful attitude will get you through the most difficult situations. [2] If you have never done this, give it a try and see!

My father was a quiet man and kept more to himself. After he passed away in 2018 from cancer, a member of our church came and said to me with tears in her eyes, "Your father was a quiet man that often got overlooked." She said, "He would stand in the corner, but if I said hello and acknowledged him, he would smile and say, 'You are the only one who said hi to me today.'" When I heard this, I wanted to cry, but it reminds me of so many people that may feel the same way. Maybe you have felt like you are in the shadows amongst the crowd. Maybe you have felt overlooked and at times have not been seen.

However, the truth is God sees you and loves you, even if others do not see you. He sees the beauty in you, the great characteristics you have, and thinks, "You are the best thing since sliced bread!" He looks at you through eyes of mercy, love, and kindness, not with judgment or criticism.

> God sees you and loves you, even if others may not see you

He loves you with a deeper love than can be imagined and says, "You are my beautiful child, you are perfect in every way, and I love you."

Have you ever walked down the halls of your workplace or within your church and taken time to complement those that are around you? When you see someone you know, do you often have an encouraging word that can lift their spirits? Many times, we may not realize it, but our words can make a difference in the lives of others. Saying things as simple as, "You look nice today, that's a beautiful color on you," or "It's great to see you," can make all the difference in the world. I encourage you today to take the time to speak life to those that surround you. Your simple words of encouragement and love can make a huge impact in the lives of others and God has promised to bless you for that! (2 Corinthians 1:4)

Words of Love

"If I speak in the tongues of men or angels but do not have love, I am only a resounding gong or a clanging cymbal. If I have the gift of prophecy and can fathom all mysteries and all knowledge, and if I have a faith that can move mountains, but do not have love, I am nothing. If I give all I possess to the poor and give over my body to hardship that I may boast, but do not have love, I gain nothing" (1 Corinthians 13: 1-3 NIV).

Having love is the most important quality that God wants us to have. He is saying that love is above every kind of spiritual gifting, above prophecy, above faith and all charity work. If we do not have a true love for people, our "Christianity" is not genuine and is a waste of God's time. God is love, and He has displayed His love throughout the Bible. He was compassionate to the adulterous woman that was getting ready to be stoned.

He allowed a woman, a known sinner within the town, to kiss and cry at his feet and wipe Him with her hair. While others looked at this woman in disgust, God chose to forgive and love her instead (Luke 7:38-39). Jesus also decided to eat dinner at Zacchaeus' house, a chief tax collector who was rich from cheating others out of their money. This man's heart was changed after one encounter with the Lord. Zacchaeus's heart was not changed by

149

Jesus's judgment and criticism over his sin. Rather it was the love that Christ showed him by choosing to eat with someone of his kind. Jesus was very loving and forgiving to all those that came across his path and His heart was moved to compassion for each of them.

This is the kind of God that we serve. A God that loves us, and sees us when we feel invisible. A God who comes after us when we have lost our way, and a God that forgives us and died on the cross to save us so that one day, we can be with Him in glory. The Bible says that God is love and He communicated His love to us by dying on the cross for our sins. John 3:16 says, "God so loved the world that He gave His only son, that whoever believes in Him would not perish but have everlasting life." He humbled himself enough to die for you and me because He loves us and wants us to have everlasting life and live with Him in paradise.

> John 3:16 says, "God so loved the world that He gave His only son, that whoever believes in Him would not perish but have everlasting life."

Christ tells us that "love is patient, love is kind *and* thoughtful, it is not jealous *or* envious; does not brag, nor is proud or arrogant. It is not rude; it is not self-seeking; it is not provoked [nor overly sensitive and easily angered]; it does not take into account a wrong *endured*. It does not rejoice at injustice but rejoices with the truth [when right and truth prevail]. Love bears all things [regardless of what comes], believes all things [looking for the best in each one], hopes all things [remaining steadfast during difficult times] and endures all things [without weakening]."

Love never fails [it never fades nor ends] and is above all things. [1] In essence, God is saying that love covers every kind of wrong that has been done to us. This may be very difficult to hear if you have been abandoned, abused either physically or emotionally, or hurt in various ways. Even still, God is here to help you through the pain if you allow Him to. Speaking and behaving in love is not always easy to do. The truth is, it can be very difficult to do; however, if we are open to God's guidance and His direction, He will help us to get there one step at a time. I have felt that in my life, I have made several mistakes in this area. I may have spoken when I should have stayed quiet, or said something at the heat of the moment, but I am so glad that God is a God of second chances.

Even if we fall in various ways, He is right there to pick us up. Giving God all your pain and opening the door to your heart will allow God to come in and heal you of your past hurts and sorrows. When you do this, you are taking one step forward, breaking off the chains that bind you, and coming into the deep love that God has for you. You will then start to notice a change in your behavior; next, your attitude; and then your words. The Bible says, "Out of the abundance of the heart, the mouth speaks" (Luke 6:45). When you are filled with God, the people around you will know it and their spirits will be lifted up by what God has done in your life.

Words of Affirmation

Words of affirmation are sincere words of appreciation, praise, or words that make people feel better. Speaking words that are positive, kind, and encouraging almost always brings a smile to a person's face. We have to admit, as humans, we all love when people say positive or good things about us or to us. Affirming someone not only makes them feel better, but it also makes us feel better. I have worked in many hospitals where there are so many people carrying burdens that are difficult for them to bear. It is pretty easy to see when people are feeling down or unhappy, but it only takes one or two words to bring a smile to their faces. It could be as simple as saying,

"Good morning, it's great to see you, hope you have a nice day," or even as simple as giving someone a smile. These small gestures may brighten someone's day and make you feel happy within yourself. Proverbs 11:25 says, "The one who blesses others is abundantly blessed; those who help others are helped" (MSG). When you bless others with either your words or actions you are impacting their lives for the better, and God has promised to bless you. [1]

In your marriages or with your kids you are making deposits into their lives on a daily basis. We all have emotional bank accounts and have the option to make deposits or withdrawals from that account. For example, in marriage, you can choose to use your words and actions to fill up your account or deplete it. Making a deposit into your marriage will only make your love and future stronger.

> The fruit of the Spirit is love, joy, peace, patience, kindness, goodness, gentleness, and faithfulness (Galatians 5:22)

Examples of deposits are words or phrases like, "You're very special to me and I thank God for you every day." "You are very beautiful or handsome." "Thank you for all the hard work that you do for us, I appreciate it." With your children, you can say, "I am so proud of you." "You are going to do great things for God one day." "You're pretty smart yourself." Making deposits in an individual's life makes them feel loved, special, and affirmed.

The fruit of the Spirit is love, joy, peace, patience, kindness, goodness, gentleness, and faithfulness (Galatians 5:22). When we have God's Spirit living within us, we often exude these characteristics from our hearts. We may not be these types of fruit every moment, but through God's changing power within us, we are becoming closer to these characteristics as we continue to grow and mature in Him.

When you begin to exhibit these fruits, eventually it works its way towards your mouth, and what's on the inside of you will come out of you. We are not often born with these qualities, but the Holy Spirit will begin to work in us and change us to be more like Jesus. Jesus Christ has exhibited all of these fruits through His character and God has asked that we become more and more like Him.

Just as we have affirmed others, we have to take time to affirm ourselves. Many of us may have grown up in a dysfunctional home where it was the opposite of a positive environment. So naturally, we have a negative internal dialogue, because that is what we have been continually exposed to over time. As a result, we can have negative thoughts that come to us on an unconscious level. However, we have to fight against that and do the opposite, which is to take time out of our day to affirm ourselves. Taking time out to affirm ourselves is the most important investment that you and I can make in our lives.

Start with making a short positive affirmation about yourself three times a day. Our minds are most receptive to positive words in the morning and at night, where we are not rushed or drifting off to sleep. You can start by saying, "I am a child of God and God loves me. I am strong, I am highly favored by God, I can do all things through Christ who strengthens me," and so on... You can also take a moment in the middle of the day to connect your emotions with your words as well. Start making a practice of this daily, and before you know it you will start to see small changes in your thinking that will happen subconsciously. This will move you closer to having a positive self-image, which is what God wants for you. I believe this will change your life and help you get to where you want to be!

Healing for Your Body, Mind, Soul, and Spirit

I heard a story of a woman who was sexually abused by her close relatives. She was only a young girl that was innocent in character and behavior, and she was hurt on many levels. Her hurt ran deep, affecting every area of her life. She was not only wounded physically, but she was also wounded emotionally, mentally, and spiritually. Eventually, she was able to escape that environment as she grew older, but she was completely broken within. Psychologists and counselors could only go so far. She needed deeper healing, and that healing was for her soul.

At first, she did not know where to begin, but she knew that she loved God and needed to turn to Him to heal her pain. She must have thought, "Where was God when

I was suffering? Why did He allow this to happen?" However, the truth is God does not bring evil upon us but the enemy does. It is the work of Satan that causes death and destruction, suffering and pain, which is the opposite of what God came to do for us (James 10:10-12). Often, we can look at the person that abused us and hate them; however, it is the enemy's work through them that has caused our pain.

The Bible says, "We do not fight against flesh and blood enemies, but rather evil rulers and authorities of the unseen world. Against mighty powers in this dark world and evil spirits in the heavenly places" (Ephesians 6:12 NLT). The enemy is the one who enters into a person's heart and leads them to sin, causing them to reap destruction in their own lives and the lives of others. Yet, our fight is not with God but with Satan.

Eventually, that woman decided to turn to God's word for her health and healing, and God took what the enemy meant for evil and turned it for her good. He gave her a double portion for her shame, her loss, and pain (Isaiah 61:7). Now this woman speaks openly and honestly about her past, and she is being used for God in various ways and is a light to all those who meet her. Jesus said, "'For I know the plans that I have for you,'" declares the LORD, "'plans to prosper you and not to harm you, plans to give you hope and a future'" (Jeremiah 29:11). God plans to bring us hope and a future, health, healing, and wholeness. His word is like a healing balm. Whatever areas that you are hurting in or may have been bruised by, God can heal you (Jeremiah 30:17).

Whether it is healing in your mind, body, soul, or spirit, the Lord is ready to receive you into His arms and heal every area of your life. The Bible says, "The Lord hears His people when they call to Him for help. He rescues them from all their troubles. The Lord is close to the brokenhearted and He rescues those who are crushed in spirit." We may face many troubles, but the Lord promises to come to the rescue each time (Psalms 34:17-20). God wants to restore your health and heal your wounds. He is the author of all good things, while Satan is the author of all bad things (James 1:17). Every good gift and every perfect gift is from above, coming down from the Father of Lights, with whom there is no variation or shadow and no change (James 1:17).

> God wants to restore your health and heal your wounds.

We are to lift our voices to God and speak to Him about our needs. Even if it means that you need to sit down and pour out your hearts before God to receive your healing. There may be times when you do not see a change in your situation and feel that your situation looks hopeless, but God does not want you to give up but to persist in prayer even when the situation appears bleak. Instead, we are to come to Him with faith and a belief that He will answer our prayers.

Hebrews 11:6 says, "But without faith, it is impossible to [walk with God and] please Him, for whoever comes [near] to God must believe that God exists and that He rewards those who [earnestly and diligently] seek Him." There is a reward that is available to us, if we believe God and persist in our prayers and actions to receive the answer we are looking for.

God has no favorites; He does not favor one person more than the other. Instead, He is loving, compassionate, and opens His arms wide to all people. He wants you to be healed, He wants you to be whole and to be happy. Throughout the Bible many scriptures tell us that God wants us to be joyful in all circumstances for this is His will for us. [1] The enemy may take his best shot at us to destroy us or bring us down in some way, but God wants to bring us life, healing, and hope. Jeremiah 33:6 says, "Nevertheless, I will bring health and healing to it; I will heal my people and will let them enjoy abundant peace and security."

Jesus went about healing everyone that wanted to be healed. A vast crowd brought to him people who were lame, blind, crippled, those who couldn't speak, and many others. They laid them before Jesus, and He healed them all (Matthew 15:30). Do you need emotional, physical, mental, psychological, or spiritual healing today? If so, reach out to God, talk to Him, and allow Him to heal the areas that are broken within you and in need of the Master's touch. He has promised to help you as you take the first step and receive His healing.

Speak Healing Scriptures

One of the best ways to encourage ourselves is to remind ourselves of God's promises and keep them at the forefront of our prayers. Reminding God of His promises does not mean that we forgot them, but rather it builds our faith and reminds us that God can be trusted to keep His word. Speaking healing Scriptures may require that we take the time to turn off the TV or social media and instead spend time in God's word that reminds us that healing is possible and available to us. When you feel overwhelmed with health problems, bad news, and things that are beyond your control, it is important to turn to God's word for supernatural strength and daily direction.

Healing for yourself comes through faith, and faith comes by hearing the word of God (Romans 10:17). When we speak God's word over and over again about a situation, something begins to take root in our spirits, and our faith assuredly begins to

> *Healing for yourself comes through faith, and faith comes by hearing the word of God (Romans 10:17).*

grow. When I was going through a rough season in my life, I would cry out to the Lord and remind Him of His promises. This helped me tremendously because it allowed me to get out all of my pent-up emotions and leave them at the feet of Jesus. God says, "Call upon me and I will answer you and show you great and mighty things that you do not know" (Jeremiah 33:3). So, I would cry out to God and quote his word by saying,

> *"God, Your word says that If I cry out to You, You will answer me and show me great and mighty things that I do not know about. Lord, I need you right now. I need Your help in this situation to make a way when there seems to be no way. Your word says that I should ask and keep on asking and it will be given to me (Matthew 7:7). So, Lord, I ask You right now, I ask that You meet my need. It is Your will that I will be healed, it is Your will that I will be made whole, it is Your will that I have abundant life. God, I ask You to meet this need, and I thank You for the answer. I believe in You, I trust You, and know that You are working all things out for my good, In Jesus name, I pray. Amen"*

Taking time to pour out your heart to God is like getting rid of all the built-up emotion and pain and laying them on God's shoulders to carry. It's almost like you have a heavy weight on your body and suddenly you throw that weight upon Jesus. That is what it is meant when the word of God says to cast your care upon Him, for He cares for you (1 Peter 5:7). Jesus cares and loves you and never meant for you to carry around burdens and heavy weights that you cannot carry. Instead, He tells us do not worry or be anxious about tomorrow and just trust Him. The truth is, our situation cannot be changed with worry, anxiety, or stress, but rather with God's help. Spend time in God's presence, memorize scripture, and recite all of God's promises over your life!

Speaking Healing Scriptures Continued...

Often people struggle with various kinds of sickness that can be devastating. Speaking healing scriptures strengthens us on the inside. When you come into agreement with God's word and say what He says about healing, you become one step closer to receiving the healing you so desperately need. The Bible says, "It is God's will to heal us" (Jeremiah 30:17, Isaiah 53:5).

I want to share a few scriptures with you that have helped encourage me and you can declare over your life. If you need to do this daily for it to get into your spirit and increase your faith, then do so. When you continue to recite God's word over your illness or any area in your life, your faith will begin to grow and you will start to see changes in your health, mind, and soul. You can begin by saying:

1. "Heal me, O Lord, and I shall be healed; save me, and I shall be saved: for You are the one I praise" (Jeremiah 17:14).

2. "O Lord my God, I cried to you for help, and you have healed me" (Psalm 30:2).

3. "Lord, You said that You 'will restore health to me; and your wounds I will heal,' declares the Lord" (Jeremiah 30:17).

4. "Lord, Your words said, 'Great crowds came to You, bringing with them the lame, the blind, the crippled, the mute, and many others, and they put them at Your feet, and You healed them all.'" Jesus went about healing *all* those who were afflicted (Matthew 15:30).

5. "Lord, You said, '"Fear not; for I am with you: be not dismayed; for I am your God: I will strengthen you; yea, I will help you; yea, I will uphold you with my right hand of righteousness'" (Isaiah 41:10).

6. "O Lord my God, I cried to You for help, and You have healed me" (Psalm 30:2).

7. "Lord, You said, '"You will meet all my needs according to the riches of His glory in Christ Jesus'" (Philippians 4:19).

8. "Lord, You said, '"With long life you will satisfy me and show me your salvation'" (Psalm 91:16).

9. "Lord, You said, "'You will honor Your promises in your written word for You will look over Your word to perform it'" (Jeremiah 1:12).

10. "Lord, You said, "'I will bring health and healing to you; I will heal My people and will let them enjoy abundant peace and security'" (Jeremiah 33:6).

11. "Lord, You said, "'If my people, who are called by My name, will humble themselves and pray and seek My face and turn from their wicked ways, then I will hear from heaven, and I will forgive their sin and will heal their land. Now my eyes will be open and my ears attentive to the prayers offered in this place'" (2 Chronicles 7:14-15).

12. "Lord, You said, "'You were wounded for my transgressions, bruised for my iniquities; The chastisement of my peace *was* upon you, and by your stripes [I was already] healed!!'" (Isaiah 53:5).

Lord, I receive this and I believe you! For You are faithful to answer me when I call on You and faithful to keep Your promises toward me. Thank You.

You can speak God's word or healing scriptures throughout the day. When you walk to work, in the shower, when you drive, etc. We build ourselves up when we speak and keep God's word at the forefront of our lives. God sees your tears and hears your cries and His arms are open wide to receive you. Tell your needs to the one that is faithful to answer and He will do what His word promises that He will do!

SECTION III

DECLARE YOUR FUTURE

CHAPTER **13**

Speak it into Existence

In Genesis, it says, "In the beginning, God created the heavens and the earth. The earth was formless and void and the darkness over the surface was deep, and God spoke and said, 'Let there be light,' and there was light" (Genesis 1:3 NIV). He then spoke again and created the earth and everything in it, and yet, in the end, He created his final masterpiece which is you and I. God loved us so much that He created us and gave us life. He used His words to create good things and through this, we have great power. The Master of the Universe does not want us to speak words of death but rather words of life. Every time God spoke about something, He did not use words of defeat and discouragement, but rather words of power and strength.

When God created the world, He called into existence something that never existed. He commanded that things appear when they were never there. You may be in a situation that looks dark and hopeless, but God has given you the authority to speak to that darkness and command it to become light. Speak out your desired result and pray in faith. If you are sick, speak to that sickness and command and declare your healing, even if you see nothing change in your circumstances.

It is not God's will for you and me to sit idly by and watch darkness overtake us. We have been given the authority to speak to areas of our lives that seem hopeless or dead and command them to live again. Jesus did not come for us to walk around gloomy, depressed, and in despair. No, the Bible says that "Jesus came to give us life and life more abundantly" (John 10:10). What does abundant life mean to you? Abundant life means more than enough, overflowing in proportion, a superabundance of joy, peace, strength, and God's presence.

God wants good things for us and wants His children to use the power and authority that he has given you to call forth things that be not, as though they were (Romans 4:17). By doing this, you are using your faith and believing God for change that you may need or desire in your life. You may need God's help in your home with your finances, or need healing in some way. God says to you today that He wants and desires for you to have what you need (James 5:14-15, Jeremiah 33:6).

> Let the weak say I am strong

The Lord says, "Let the weak say I am strong" (Joel 3:10) He did not say, "Let the weak say I am weak," instead, He wants us to speak to that broken area and command healing. That means we have to take a position of authority over the spirits of darkness and spiritual forces of evil, and take a stand in our faith and get back what the enemy has stolen from us. If the enemy has stolen your health, shattered your home, and wrecked your family, God does not want you to sit idly by and say, "Oh woe is me, my family is in pieces, I have lost my health, I have nothing... gosh, why has this happened to me?" No, instead he wants you to rise up and defeat the enemy!

Imagine with me, if someone came into your home in the middle of the night and was attempting to hurt your loved one. Something on the inside of you would RISE UP and attempt to master that evil person. You may even scream with an outlandish cry, "NOOO!!" and do your best to fight off the intruder that has invaded your home. You are to respond in the same way when Satan comes to steal, kill, and destroy you. [1]

The Bible says that we are to put on the full armor of God, so that we can take our stand against the devil's schemes. "For your struggle is not against flesh and blood, but against the rulers, against the authorities, against the powers of this dark world and the spiritual forces of evil in the heavenly realms." [2]

When the enemy comes our way, we have to fight him with our sword. This sword is the word of God. In order to fight we have to read and meditate on God's word until it gets down into our spirits and we know them for ourselves. So, when Satan whispers words of worry, fear or doubt, find verses in the Bible that will contradict his lies, and God says when you do this, he must flee from you! (James 4:7)

No matter what it is, or what you have been through, God wants you to keep standing. He has already given you the victory over your situation. Now stand up, fight him with God's word, and after you have done all to stand, keep standing! (Ephesians 6:13).

Valley of Dry Bones

There is a story in the Bible of a man named Ezekiel. Ezekiel was given a vision by God of a valley filled with dry bones. In this valley, Ezekiel talks about how God told him to walk amongst this valley filled with dry, brittle old bones that were lifeless. *Then God said to Ezekiel, "Son of man, can these bones live?" and I, Ezekiel said, "Sovereign Lord, you alone know" (See Ezekiel 37).*

This passage is very interesting to me because God knew the answer to the question that He had asked, but He was waiting to see what Ezekiel would *say* about the problem. He wanted to know if Ezekiel believed if these bones could live, or if he just thought that what's dead is dead and there is nothing that he could do about it.

Then God said to Ezekiel, "Prophesy to these bones and say to them, *'Dry bones, hear the word of the Lord!'* For this is what the Sovereign Lord says to these bones: *'I will make breath enter you, and you will come to life. I will attach tendons to you and make flesh come upon you and cover you with skin; I will put breath in you, and you will come to life. Then you will know that I am the Lord'"* (Ezekiel 37).

In all honesty, God could have brought the dry bones to life Himself. Instead, He tells Ezekiel to use his mouth to command that the dry bones will live again in the name, power, and authority of God. God wanted Ezekiel to do something about the dead situation. He did not want Ezekiel to sit back and say, "Oh, well there's a problem here and there's nothing we can do about it." No, instead He tells Ezekiel to do something about the problem. God tells Ezekiel that he has the power within himself to use his mouth to create change and call forth life in this valley of dry bones.

So, Ezekiel did as the Lord commanded and he spoke to those bones. He then heard a "thundering noise and a rattling of sound. Suddenly, he started to notice that the bones were coming together. Each bone was joining the other in perfect formation. He then noticed that tendons, flesh, and skin were appearing on the body. Amazing! However, he stopped because he noticed that there was no breath in them.

Then God told him, "Son of man, speak a prophetic message and say to it, this is what the Sovereign Lord says: 'Come, breath from the four winds, and breathe into these dead bodies, that they may live again.' So, Ezekiel prophesied as God commanded him, and breath came into all the bodies, and they stood up like a vast army!" (Ezekiel 37).

It is amazing to me that Ezekiel was able to call forth life into something that was dead. Through the power of God, this young man was able to do the impossible! His words had creative power and he was able to call forth something that seemed lifeless and unimaginable. However, God was showing Ezekiel that all things are possible to those that believe (Mark 9:23).

In the same way, God is telling you and me that we also carry the same power with our words and faith. Jesus told his disciples, "Surely, I tell you, if you speak to that mountain, and say be lifted up and thrown into the sea, and do not doubt but believe in your heart that is done, you will have what you say." God has given us power through His written word to speak to those dry, barren, and dead areas of our lives and cause hope, joy, and life to spring forth.

He has given us the power to "heal the sick, raise the dead, cleanse the lepers, and drive out demons" (Matthew 10:8). When you are sick, speak out and say, "In the name of Jesus Christ I declare that I am healed. The Bible says, 'By His stripes, I am healed' and I command my body to straighten up and get in line with the word of God. I declare that I am healed, I am whole, and will be healthy until I die." These are examples of how to use your words to change your situation. You must believe God's words to you in order to see the miraculous happen in your life. The power of God is available to you and God wants you to use it and use it boldly! You have the power to bring forth life or death into your situation, choose life!

> *The power of God is available to you and God wants you to use it and use it boldly!*

Yes, You Can

"O LORD, you have examined my heart and know everything about me. You know when I sit down or stand up. You know my thoughts even when I'm far away. You know everything I do. You know what I am going to say even before I say it, LORD. Before a word is on my tongue, you know it completely. For you created my inmost being; you knit me together in my mother's womb. I praise you because I am fearfully and wonderfully made; your works are wonderful; I know that full well" (Psalms 139).

God told Jeremiah, "Before I formed you in your mother's womb, I knew you, before you were born, I set you apart and appointed you as a prophet to the nations" (Jeremiah 1:5).

Jeremiah was asked by the Lord to do special work. In the same way, God has set you apart for a special job that only you can do. He has gifted you with a unique character, personality, talent, and gifting that only you can offer. God did not make a mistake when He made you. You are made exactly as He called you to be and He loves you. He has a special purpose for every one of us and He wants us to be able to accomplish what He has called us to do.

Yet Jeremiah was not too sure that he could fulfill the role that God was asking him to do. Jeremiah said, Lord, "I do not know how to speak; I am too young." In essence, he was saying, "I don't think I'm qualified, I don't think I'm good enough. I have all of these obstacles in front of me that may disqualify me." However, the Lord said to him, "Do not say you are too young, because I have a plan for you. I want you to go to everyone I send you to, and say whatever I command you to. Do not be afraid because I will be with you and rescue you, and help you in your time of need" (see Jeremiah 1:7)

See, when God has a plan for us no one can stand against that. God was telling Jeremiah, "Don't say that you are not able to do something when I have said you can." Do not use your words to speak defeat and failure. Instead, think and speak words of faith and victory. God cannot use us to the fullest extent if we do not believe in ourselves and are so focused on the impossibilities rather than the possibilities through God's help.

Imagine if Jeremiah continued to say over and over again, "God, I just can't do it. I know You have told me that I can, but I just know that I will not be able to do what You are asking me to do." Then the truth is, God will not force us to do something that we do not want to do. Instead, He will appoint someone else, just as He did in the story of Elijah and Elisha. If we are not able to come into agreement with what God has in store for us, then we will miss out on the wonderful opportunities that may not come again.

Then the Lord touched Jeremiah's mouth and said, "I have put my words in your mouth. Go and use those words to uproot and destroy or to build up and plant the nations." You can be sure that whatever God has called you to do, He has promised to be with you and will equip you as you trust in Him. Jeremiah did not know how he could do what God was calling him to do. It seemed overwhelming and beyond what was comfortable for him to do.

Jeremiah was speaking all the reasons why he could not do what God was asking him to do, rather than saying all the reasons why he could do what was being asked of him. He must have thought, "There is no way I can do this. I have to give a difficult message to the Israelites that I do not think I can give; this is too hard." However, the great thing about God is that when He calls you, He will equip you for the task at hand. God touched Jeremiah's mouth and filled it with the things that He wanted Jeremiah to say.

This is similar to the life of Moses, who stuttered, and also felt he was inadequate to speak in front of the Pharaoh. There again, God filled his mouth and equipped those that He sent out. I love this about the Lord, that He does not just ask us to do something alone, but instead helps us to be able to do it. In the same way, God has given you and I the same power. You can do everything God has called you to do. He has promised to be with you and make you a light for all to see as you walk in His path and give Him glory.

Calling it Forth

God is a God that can do the supernatural.

Calling forth those things that are not as though they were puts us in a position of receiving all that God has for us to receive. Often, we look at our situation in the natural world and it looks impossible or unachievable; however, God is a God that can do the supernatural. You may look at your weak body or your child that is bedridden and stricken by disease, and the obvious is that your situation looks bleak. However, there is always hope when you believe in Jesus!

No matter what the circumstances are, we can always choose hope and joy amid our pain. When we are in situations that are painful or difficult to deal with, it is not God's will for us to get in agreement with the negative of our situation. Rather, He wants us to change and come in agreement with His words and call forth those things that are not, as though they were. You may say, "What if I pray for my child and he/she does not get better?" However, my question is, what if you pray and your child does get better? It is always better to do your very best and go after your miracle rather than sitting around and waiting for God to do it for you.

The women with the issue of blood had to go after her miracle to receive healing. She did all that she could do in the physical realm and asked God to do what she could not do in the supernatural realm. When we are weak the Bible instructs us to say that we are strong (Joel 3:10). Get in agreement with God's word and speak life over your dead situation. God never instructs the weak to say, "I am weak," or the poor to say, "Yeah, I am pretty poor and there is not much I can do about it." Instead, He wants us to speak in faith and say the opposite of what we see, and move in the direction that we seek.

When you are sick, start telling other people, "God is healing me, I feel better and better with each day. I am healed in Jesus' name and I will do what He has planned for me to do." Or, when you are in debt, start telling others if they ask, "I am debt free, God has helped me and I have my finances in order and I thank God for that!" This may be difficult at first, but the more you say it, the more faith will begin to arise within you. As you speak healing, healing will rise. When you speak victory, you will start to feel more victorious. In the same way, if you speak defeat, you will start to feel more defeated. No matter how bleak your situation looks, God is still on the throne and can do the impossible for you. Start speaking forth in faith even though you do not see the answer to your need.

This was made evident in the life of Abraham. God called Abraham a father of many nations, even though there was no hope that Abraham would ever have any children. Nonetheless, he believed God's word and continued to have hope. Romans 4:16-17 tells us that even though God foretold to Abraham things he could not see in the present, his faith is what brought about his miracle. If God can call forth things that "be not as though they were" then we who are made in the same image of God can do the very same thing. Romans 8:11; Romans 8:10-20).

God blessed Abraham by telling him, "You believed in my promises, and My word to you, against all hope. You believed me even when it seemed impossible and others said it could not be done. You believed even when your body was aging, dead within, and unable to produce a child. You believed in faith and trusted My words, and that is why I have made you the father of many nations." God told Abraham, "Because of your faith in me, you will see, apprehend, and receive all that has been promised to you" (Romans 4: 18-22). God told Abraham that he would be "the father of many nations," even though there was no sign of it.

Imagine for a second if God called you a mighty warrior, but you felt quite the opposite instead. Perhaps you were skinny looking, of average height, and did not "look" like a mighty warrior. Nonetheless, God decided to bring a woman into your life who is now your wife. God placed in this woman an ability to see beyond the surface, and she saw greatness in you.

She decides to come into agreement with what God said about you, even though you cannot see it nor believe it for yourself. What if she said daily, in the morning when you woke up and throughout the day, "Good morning, mighty warrior, would you like some breakfast today?" Or what if you came home from work and again, she said, "Mighty warrior, can you give me a hand by getting that heavy box down from that shelf?" Or, "Mighty warrior, I agree with God, I see you able to do what God says you can do. You are strong, skillful and ready for anything!"

> *What is impossible for man is possible with God (Luke 18:27)*

You would find that as a man your faith would begin to rise and your belief in who you are would begin to change. Even though you may not have believed this at first, your wife was "calling forth things which were not there, as though they were." She came into agreement with what God said about you in His word and she spoke life into you.

Calling those things that be not as though they were, is getting a revelation in your spirit that you can have whatever you say you can have. (Mark 11:23). Paul says, "Because I believed God's words, I have already spoken it." In the same way, when you believe God for what you need, you will go ahead and talk to others like you already have it (2 Corinthians 4:13 NIV). God puts our destiny before us and gives us dreams, visions, and desires to stir up our faith and believe for the miraculous. It is impossible to receive the miraculous if your mouth and mind do not come into agreement with what God says you can do. I encourage you today to pray, call forth your miracle, and believe God for the impossible situations in your life.

What Do You Say?

"Then God looked over all he had made, and he saw that it was very GOOD" (Genesis 1:13). In the beginning of the Bible, we see that whatever God had created He thought was good. Genesis 1:18 says that God saw that the light He spoke into existence was good. He separated the dry ground from water, the light from darkness, and created all living things above and beneath and then again stepped back and said, "This is good." With every part of creation, I can imagine God smiling and saying, "Wow, that's pretty amazing as well, if I have to say so myself." It's interesting to me that God did not step back, scratch his head, and say, "Darn it, that's terrible, I can't believe I did that. I'm so dumb, and here I go again, making another mistake." No, God was just the opposite.

Throughout the Bible, God always speaks in a tone of love, a positive spirit, and focuses on everything good. God is good, and what He says about you is even better. He says that you are beautiful. He says that you are unique, special, and one of a kind. God says that you are His masterpiece and perfect in every way. He did not make a mistake when He made you (Ephesians 2:10). He made you in His very own image and that means you came out just perfect. [1] God says that He loves you and He has a great plan in store for you. He has plans to prosper you and not to harm you, He has plans to give you hope and a future (Jeremiah 29:11). The Word of God says, "The enemy comes to steal, kill, and destroy you, but God came to give you life and life more abundantly" (John 10:10)

> "The enemy comes to steal, kill, and destroy you, but God came to give you life and life more abundantly"
> (John 10:10)

There may be times that you may go through situations that did not turn out just as you imagined. Maybe someone walked out on you, or you were diagnosed with a terminal condition. Maybe you are even facing a situation now that seems bigger than you. Instead of feeling down and depressed, God wants you to stand up, be bold, and encourage yourself in the Lord (see Joshua 7:10). When you feel as if everything is coming against you, and your situation seems overwhelming, that is the time to dig your heels into the ground, trust God, and stand despite what you see happening around you.

This is what David had to do when he made a mistake. David had led his men into battle while leaving all the women and children in Ziglag behind, defenseless and without protection. When David and the men returned home to Ziglag they found that all of the women and children were taken captive by their enemy (see 1 Samuel 30 AMP). With this realization, David and his men were distraught and fell on the floor sobbing and wept aloud until they could weep no more. Everything was gone, all that was important to them was stripped away. While looking around at the destruction around them, the men began to grow more angry with David and were talking about stoning him. I can imagine one of the men saying, "It's all his fault, if he would not have led us out into battle then we could have protected our wives and children, but now they are gone."

David began to hear them talking about stoning him. Even though he was distressed and hurt, the Bible says that David strengthened and encouraged himself in the Lord (1 Samuel 30:6 AMP). David asked God if he should go after the enemy, and God said yes and promised him success in the battle. David and his men recovered everything that the Amalekites had taken, including his two wives. Nothing was missing: young or old, boy or girl, plunder or anything else they had taken. David had recovered all that was lost!

Even though David had made a mistake, he offered himself grace and forgiveness. Do you do the same for yourself? When you try your best at a project and it does not succeed, do you start thinking negatively and berate yourself with your words? Or do you do the opposite and say to yourself, "I will keep trying and not give up. Even though things have not turned out the way I expected, I will keep giving it my best shot, and I know I will have the victory."

What do you say about your situation? What you say about yourself and to yourself matters. Decide today to say what God says about you. He forgives you when you make mistakes, He is for you and not against you, and He is gentle and kindhearted. He does not look down on you, scold you, and beat you over the head when you don't perform perfectly. Instead, His arms are open wide to you today, and He says that you are His child, you are perfect in every way, and He loves you. Today, say with me, "I am smart, I am beautiful, I am anointed, I am equipped, I am strong, I can do all things through Christ who strengthens me." [2]

"I am healthy, I will live out my days in victory, and most of all, I am loved." Come into agreement with what God says about you and when you do this, you will be able to enjoy the life that He desires to give you.

CHAPTER 14

A Heart of Thankfulness

I can remember a time during my childhood when I had a best friend and we were inseparable. Jenny and I did everything together. We were neighbors, went to the same school, talked every day, and were best of friends. Until one day another girl moved into our neighborhood named Tina. Tina knew Jenny and I were best friends and she was not very happy about the idea. I was open to having a third friend join Jenny and I; however, I could quickly sense that this was not the idea Tina had in mind.

They were both of one race and I was of the other, which made it even more awkward. Even though Jenny and I had a long history of friendship, it was quickly dissolving with the addition of our new company. Tina tried everything to separate us, by excluding me from their discussions, walking away with Jenny when I would come by, and laughing even though there was nothing funny to laugh about. Although this bothered me, I still tried my best to maintain my friendship as much as I could, but the more I tried the more it seemed as if things were getting worse.

Life quickly started to become more difficult and it became unbearable for me to go to school with them daily, because their behaviors were very similar to bullying, but just in a female way. I am not sure if you remember being in that 11-13 age group where friendship, being accepted, fitting in, and finding your identity were big deals. These adolescent years were very difficult years for me. Everywhere I would turn, there they were, snickering, laughing, and attempting to make me feel worse.

I felt like my friend Jenny was brainwashed and I had no control over it. I then began to cry and pray hard. Jenny, Tina, and I all lived in the same neighborhood and in the same zip code, which meant that not only would we go to middle school together, but high school as well, because we were in the same school district. This would mean I would see them daily for years, which was something I just could not bear. When I thought about this, I felt mortified and did not know what to do.

I began to talk to God about it daily and I cried out to Him for an answer (see Jeremiah 33:3). I remember one day I cried so much that my pillow felt soaked and I said, "God, I don't know what else to do, or how I can fix this problem. I just can't do this every day, it's too much for me to bear." I then said in a quiet muffled voice, "The only thing I can think of is if someone moves away..." With my eyes full of tears, I put my head down on the pillow and thought, "I just don't know what else to do, God, please help me." Then I closed my eyes and slept.

What happened next was miraculous and something I want to share with as many people as I can. Exactly *one week* after my prayer, my friend Jenny came up to me while I was out in my driveway getting the mail. She said with a sad face, "Julie, I have some bad news to tell you. My dad just got a new job in Missouri and my dad told us that we will have to move there." My mouth dropped open; you should have seen me! I was stunned, speechless, and shocked all at the same time! Oh, my goodness, I could not believe my ears. Is this happening, is this true?

My heart jumped with joy on the inside of me, but I had to contain myself. Not only was I happy that there was a resolution to my problem, but greater than that, God heard me and answered my prayer!!! I felt that I shared my heart with God, and He made a way just exactly as I had prayed! What an awesome God we serve. God made a way when there was an impossible situation in front of me. He made a way when what seemed like a mountain that was once immovable now became a pile of rocks and rubble that lay like a heap in front of me.

I was so thankful to God for answering my prayer and for just taking the time out to listen to me. He showed me that He sees me, He hears me, and most of all, that He loves me. He loved me enough to answer even my smallest concerns. He can do the same thing for you. When

> God hears you and will answer your prayers

people come against you, criticize and put you down, God will defend you and be there right when you need Him most.

Trying to contain myself, I then asked her when she was planning to move. She told me that they had to move soon and it would most likely be in two weeks. This was bittersweet, I was shocked because it was so soon. Deep down I felt kind of sad to see her go because of our long history of friendship, but I knew it was for the better. This was a miracle, my first miracle! God lovingly helped me through a situation that looked hopeless! God showed me His goodness and grace and made a way for me even when the road ahead looked bleak. I talked daily to God and He heard my prayer and delivered me, and I will be forever thankful to Him for that.

God is willing and available to help you in your time of need, just as He has done for me. David said, "I cried out to the Lord, and He heard me and answered my cry" (Psalms 120:1, Jonah 2:2). If there is something that you are dealing with and cannot seem to find an answer to, talk to God. Tell Him about all your problems, tell Him about your needs, and believe in Him for the answer. God hears your cry and has promised that He will wipe away your tears. Go to Him with your problems, trust Him, and watch Him do miracles for you! (Job 5:8-9; Jeremiah 33:27).

Be Thankful and Say So

We have so much to be thankful for. Thankful for our families, friends, homes, and most importantly, the breath in our lungs and the ability to wake up every day and to get out of bed. If you think about it, God has done so much for you and I and has provided for our every need. Being thankful means we appreciate God for all the things He has given us, whether it is big or small. However, oftentimes when we get used to having everything we need, we tend to take things for granted and forget the giver of all good things.

Having a grateful heart begins with having a humble heart. To be thankful we have to be able to come into a position of lowering our pride, bowing down before God in reverence and humbleness, and with an honest heart say, "Thank You." This is what King David did, and that is why God called David a man

> Having a grateful heart begins with having a humble heart.

after His own heart. Even though King David suffered in many ways and made a few mistakes, he always humbled himself, repented of his sins, and sought any way to please God's heart. In the book of Psalms, David continuously talks about his thanksgiving to God. He writes in Psalms 103:1-4 (ESV)

> "Bless the Lord, O my soul,
> and all that is within me,
> bless His holy name!
> Bless the Lord, O my soul,
> and forget not all His benefits,
> who forgives all your iniquity,
> who heals all your diseases,
> who redeems your life from the pit,
> and crowns you with steadfast love and mercy"

David is saying, "God, with everything in me, and with every fiber of my being, I praise You. I thank You for forgiving me of all my sins and healing me from all my diseases. Without You and without Your presence, where would I be? I will never forget all the wonderful things You have done for me. Due to Your lovingkindness, I do not have to go down into a pit. Your love, mercy, and forgiveness has been extended to me. Without You, I would be nothing, yet You loved me despite everything I have done wrong and I am eternally grateful for that."

Over and over again we see David expressing a heart full of thanks, worship, and love towards God. As a child of God, we also have so much to be thankful for. The Bible says, "Let the redeemed of the Lord say so" (Psalms 107:2). If you have been redeemed, saved, healed, set free from bondages and strongholds, the Bible encourages us to talk and tell others about it, and most of all, thank God for it.

Jesus offered us salvation by dying on the cross for all of our sins so that we would ultimately be forgiven and be able to live with Him in eternity forever. John 3:16 says, "For God so loved the world that He gave his only begotten Son, that whosoever believeth in Him should not perish, but have everlasting life." Jesus died to give you an abundant life, and he wants you to have a hope and a future (Jeremiah 29: 11).

If God has been faithful to you in any area of your life, or has been good to you, I encourage you to lift up your voice and thank Him for the answer and His faithfulness towards you. As you do this, I believe God will be looking down from heaven, leaning down towards you with a big warm smile on His face and say, "I love you, my precious child, and you are very welcome."

A Joyful Heart

Having a joyful heart means putting a smile on your face, showing those pearly white teeth, and giving God some praise for all that he has done for you. Psalms 100:4-5 says, "*Enter His gates with thanksgiving, enter His courts with praise. Give thanks to Him and bless His name. For the Lord is good and His love endures forever, and His faithfulness to all generations.*" God wants us to be joyful and have a glad heart. We may go through situations that we don't understand, or a plan does not go as expected. However, God says, "Count it all joy when you face various trials

> *The Lord will use what the enemy meant for evil and turn it for your good.*

and tribulations, because those trials test your faith and that test of faith will bring out endurance and patience" (James 1:2-8).

Now, if you allow patience to have its full work in you, then you will be fully developed, perfect, and lacking nothing. Even when the enemy tries to get you down and discouraged, the Lord will use what the enemy meant for evil and turn it for your good. Going through tough times is not easy; trust me, I know! However, God has promised to work it out for your good and to make you stronger so that you can face anything that comes your way.

A diamond is one of the rarest, best known, and most sought-after gemstones in the world. Diamonds are typically made from carbon that lies below the earth, and through volcanic eruptions comes bursting out of the ground and onto the surface. [1] Before being found amid dirt and rubble, a diamond has to undergo an immense amount of high heat temperatures and flames to come out as a shining, brilliant gem that is sought out by millions around the world.

In the same way, we may go through a time of extreme heat, testing our faith, and face tribulations of all kinds. However, God always encourages us not to give up our hope and our faith in Him, but to trust Him in all things. Proverbs 3:5-6 says, "Trust in the Lord with all your heart and lean not on your understanding. In all your ways acknowledge Him and He will direct your paths.

This was the case for Paul and Silas when they were thrown into prison and had to endure hardships of all kinds. The jail cell was dirty, rusty, and old.

> Our victory comes from being joyful amidst a dark situation.

Other prisoners were yelling, cursing, and most probably not saying the kindest of words. Paul and Silas were thrown into prison not for committing murder, for stealing goods, or committing a grand crime, rather they were thrown into prison for casting a demon out of a woman (Acts 16:16-40).

If you think about it, this was a good thing. A woman was set free from a burden that she had been carrying for a long time. However, the local businessmen were not happy with that, and with the help of other officials, they threw the two men into prison. Despite being arrested, beaten, and thrown into jail, both men kept a good attitude and were joyful in the midst of their dark situation.

However, Paul and Silas understood the principle that complaining, dwelling on their troubles, and having a self-pity party would not change their circumstances. Instead, they used a powerful tool of prayer and worship to give God thanks. They used their words to give God glory in any way they could. I can imagine the two singing, "We love you, Lord. Lord, we thank you for all you have done, we worship You because You are holy and worthy to be praised!"

Amid a horrible situation, their thanksgiving and worship are what opened heaven's doors for the answer. God was moved not by their complaints, but rather He was moved by their praise, prayer, and worship (Acts 16: 25-28).

At that very moment when they began to pray and sing, suddenly there was an earthquake that caused the prison doors to fly open. Paul and Silas, along with others, were able to escape and even saved the prison guard from committing suicide on their way out. God broke the shackles, freed them from their chains, and did the miraculous at the very point at which they began to thank, praise, and worship him. Their hearts of gratefulness, their words of prayer and praise, are what touched God's very heart and caused Him to move.

You may be going through a difficult situation that you have no answer for, or are facing circumstances in which you do not know what to do. However, God has the answer. In every situation, pray first, then began to praise God for the answer in advance. Even if you do not see anything happen, continue to praise Him and trust that at the right time, He will bring about a miracle. Ultimately, our prayer, praise, and a grateful heart is a recipe for miracles, and miracles are what God wants to do for you!

An Ungrateful Spirit

I had just finished teaching a Bible study in our women's group on the importance of being grateful and having a thankful heart amid *all* situations. Soon after that, I was scheduled to go to a work-related conference in the Florida Keys. While driving to the Keys I had this beautiful image in my head of what the resort would be like. I imagined great food, an amazing room, and wonderful amenities.

Not to mention that the brochure of the resort looked amazing as well, so I was excited! Driving to the Florida Keys was beautiful, but closer to the resort the roads became more narrow, isolated, and had poor lighting. There were no stores, restaurants or signs of civilization for miles leading up to the conference site. This bothered me, but I brushed it off. I finally reached my destination and it truly did look beautiful.

This was a sight to see and my hopes were up! I finally reached the front of this large resort and asked about parking and was told that the parking was off at another site, which appeared to be pretty far away. Okay, that's a little odd, but no worries! I will grab my suitcases, extra bags, and roll them over. The pavement toward the resort was very bumpy and uneven and it made the walk with my heavy luggage that much harder. I then walked into a beautiful room and it all appeared amazing. "This is going to be good," I thought. I finally reached my room to find it looked like an average room with a bed, clean sheets, and a very basic appearance, nothing very special. "This was okay," I thought, "but I'm sure there are going to be other great things to see."

This facility was beautiful and very large on the brochure, and I was excited to explore and go all around this huge resort. However, I quickly found out that it was not a location for most visitors. Rather, the majority of guests congregated only on the smaller side of the property, which is where I was. "This was a bummer," I thought. I was hoping to see all of the resort, but it was not an option, so there was not much more that I could do about it.

I then decided to go down for dinner, only to find that almost all of the open restaurants were empty, with one or two people in them and a few people gathered near the fireplace at the pool. I tried the food for myself and could see why people left the hotel to get their meals.

I then realized that I had a list in my head of all the things that were not right in the resort. My list included poor Wi-Fi connection with an inability to make telephone calls, having to eat really poor quality food at the resort, my GPS/phone services were not working even outside of the facility secondary to their Wi-Fi, having to drive for miles with no restaurant in sight, unfortunately having to watch reruns of the same shows for most of the week, and no microwave to heat my food, and the list went on...

Like many of us, it was very easy to be ungrateful when a few of the usual comforts that we normally enjoy were not there. When I realized what God was saying to me, I chuckled on the inside thinking about the fact that I just taught on being grateful in all situations and here I was complaining. I grumbled and complained and I laughed saying, "You got me, God, I didn't practice what I preached."

I could imagine Jesus smiling from heaven, winking and chucking Himself. That was a pretty good joke, if I must say so myself, and I loved that God had a sense of humor. He loved me enough and had enough grace to show me that it is important to be grateful in all things, which is something we as humans often forget. It is often easier to focus on the negative and look at what we do not have rather than what we do have. That is why it is important to stop and say thank you to God, because it not only honors Him but puts us in a position to receive His blessings.

As Jesus was traveling into a village, ten men with leprosy had met Him and shouted from a distance and said, "Jesus, Master, have pity on us, have pity on us, Lord!" When Jesus saw them, he told them to go to their priest and as they went, they were cleansed of leprosy. When one man saw that he was healed, he jumped and ran back to Jesus and said in a loud voice, "Jesus, son of God, thank You so much, thank You for all that You have done for me!" He threw himself at Jesus' feet and thanked Him for his healing! Jesus then stated, "Were there not ten lepers that were cleansed, where are the other nine? Only this man has come back to say thank you, amongst the rest" (Luke 17: 11-19).

In this illustration, God is showing us that He is honored by a grateful heart and sees those who are truly thankful to him. Some get what they want and forget God, but that will rob you of your blessings. Being grateful to God is coming to Him and humbling yourself, knowing that he is the giver of every good gift and has provided for your needs thus far. Taking time to thank God for dying on the cross for us, being gracious

> Being good to others comes from a grateful heart and opens the door for God to meet all your needs,

and merciful, opens the heart of God to show you favor and allows you to experience His blessings in a greater way. I encourage you to make this a daily practice. When you do, you will begin to feel God's love and presence in a greater way.

Practical Ways to Practice Gratitude

Some ways that you can practice gratitude are to:

1. Create a Gratitude Journal
   - Setting time apart in your busy day to write down what you are thankful for. It serves as a reminder of all the good things that God has done for you. When you have times of loneliness, pain, or discouragement you can refer back to your journal and think of all the times that God has gotten you through and provided for your needs. By doing this, you will lift your spirits and get back to that place of rest, joy, and peace.

2. Practice gratitude at the same time every day
   - Take time to thank God every day, whether it be in the morning when you wake up, or before you go to bed at night. Find at least 3-5 positive things that went well for you in your day or anything you are grateful for.

   - Thank God for giving you grace even though you have made mistakes. Or, thank Him for His salvation and forgiveness of your sins and shortcomings.

3. Start appreciating not just the big things but the small things as well:
   - Good weather
   - Kids behaved today
   - Dinner turned out pretty good.
   - I did not lose my temper today, and so on...

4. Being a Blessing
- Talk to those you care about, and tell them you are grateful for them. This will not only increase your joy, but it will increase the joy of the one who hears it.

- Be a blessing to others. It is easy to fall into the trap of focusing only on ourselves rather than look for ways to bless someone else. Bless others through simple acts like:

a. Making eye contact and offering a smile to brighten someone's day
b. Paying someone a compliment - such as "I love that dress," or, "you did a good job on that project," "That's a nice color on you" - are simple expressions of love that help others to know that you see them and they matter.

Your words have the power to build others up or bring them down.

c. Wish someone a good day or simply say, "It's good to see you today."
d. Buy someone a cup of coffee or treat them to lunch
e. Pray for others, whether they are in front of you or walking beside you. You never know what they may be going through.

Your words can bless those that you come in contact with and invite God's presence into their situation.

Offering prayer, whether it be in passing, in the grocery store, or anywhere you see someone that may be hurting, would be the best thing that you could do for that person. When you bless others through various acts God will bless you in return. This can also be seen in the life of Abraham. Abraham was a humble man and always thanked God. Due to his heart, God told him, "I will make you into a great nation. I will bless you and make your name great, and you will be a blessing to others (Genesis 12:2).

God did not increase Abraham just for his own sake, but rather God wanted him to be a blessing to others. The Bible says, "The one who blesses others [whether through words or deed] is abundantly blessed; and those who help others are helped" (Proverbs 11:25 MSG). Being good to others comes from a grateful heart and opens the door for God to meet all your needs, which will ultimately increase your joy. If you have not already, I encourage you to take time and thank God for all the wonderful things He has done for you and all the things He has brought you through.

CHAPTER 15

Prophesying Your Future

Prophesying your future with your words means that you are "*speaking* your future into existence." "When you prophecy you are projecting a word into the future about your life." [1] Basically, if you seek something, then speak it into existence and call those things that be not as though they already are. (Romans 4:17). The Bible says, "Let the weak say I am strong." [1] That means when you are weak, sick, or poor, you ought to declare in advance what it is that you want to see happen. Negative words will never allow you to reach your destiny, rather it takes words of faith to help you get there.

I once heard a story from a young woman who brought her husband into the hospital because she noticed that he was suddenly incontinent and unable to control his bowels. She said initially his symptoms began when she found him doing odd things like saying he was ready to go to the store, but only came out of the house dressed in his shirt and boxers. At first, she thought it was a joke, but his symptoms only got worse. After one or two episodes of these odd behaviors, she became concerned and took him to the hospital for a check-up. When the medical report came back, she was shocked to hear that the medical team had found that her husband had a brain tumor with metastasis, along with another life-threatening virus. He was only in his early forties.

Then she went on to tell me, "You know, when my husband came to this country he would always point to old people and say, 'I never want to look like that, I'm not going to get old and decrepit. Those old people look all wrinkled and bad, I'm not going to be old.'" She said her husband would say the same thing over and over again and she would always warn him by saying, "Honey, don't say that, don't talk like that." However, he just continued repeating the same phrase over and over again. She then told me, "You know what, he said this all the time. He would make fun of those that were old and never wanted to become old, and now, look." Then she said in sadness, "Look, you see, he got what he was asking for." Unfortunately, this young man unknowingly prophesied his future and he passed away as a result. He prophesied his future in advance, and in ignorance; however, his words ultimately became his reality.

Our words have the power to affect our future potential, so we ought to pay close attention to what we say. God has given us the power to be able to call forth things even though they may not have happened as of yet. The Bible says that "we will have what we say" (Mark 11:22-25). This means that if you say, "I am coming out of debt" and work towards that goal, then believe it or not, you will be coming out. Or, if you say, "God has opened up a new door for me and I am going to have my own house one day,"

> Speak in the direction you seek

195

you are prophesying your future into existence. When you pray or ask God for something in faith, it is also important to have the corresponding action needed to get there.

> God is on your side and desires to give you good things.

It is a wonderful thing to know that no matter what your circumstances are, or where you have come from, you have the same power and ability as any other person to be all that God has created you to be. You do not have to allow your circumstances to rule over you. Instead, no matter what the problem is, God wants you to rise and come "boldly before His throne" and declare victory! (Hebrews 4:16).

God is on your side and desires to give you good things. If it is healing that you need, declare in advance that you are already healed. For example, you can say, "Lord, You said, 'By your stripes, I am healed,' then because You have said it, I believe it. I believe that over 2,000 years ago You took my shame, my sickness, my mistakes, and every sin that I have committed, and You washed me clean and you have *already healed* me. I take that healing because it is already mine" (Isaiah 53:5). If you are asking God to be debt-free, do your part and God will do His part. Start declaring in advance, "Lord, You said that you will fully supply all my needs according to Your glorious riches in Christ Jesus" (Philippians 4:13).

If you are asking God for a good mate, then declare that in due time He will bring that right person to you. Keep believing, and prophecy and declare in faith what you would like to see in your future. God is on your side, and even if it would mean that you would need to make this declaration every day, be determined that even until your last dying day this is what you will continue to do in agreement with God's word and His will for you.

When we prophesy over our future, it means that we are coming into agreement with God's words and saying what He says about our future. God wants us to prosper and He wants good things for us (3 John 1:2). He is not against you, nor is He pointing a finger at you in scorn every time you mess up. No, He loves you and forgives you when you make a mistake and is ready to help you up again.

I came from a very conservative church background growing up. I was taught to fear God rather than being taught to have a reverence of God. So, when I messed up, I would always imagine God angry at me and saying, "You messed up, you did it again." I had this view of God for so many years, until I read the *whole* Bible and realized He was nothing like that at all. Instead, God sent His son Jesus to die on the cross for us, even though He knew we would fall short. He took away our sins when He shed His blood and died on that cross for you and me. He lovingly paid the price for us, even though we did not deserve it, so that we could spend a life with Him in heaven for all eternity.

As I began to grow in my knowledge, I realized that God was nothing that I imagined Him to be. Instead, He was, and is, loving, patient, kind, gentle, faithful, forgiving, and merciful. He loves you and is rooting for you, and He wants you to prosper in every way. You have the power to prophecy into your future and take hold of what it is that you desire. Once you pray, thank God and faithfully wait

197

and expect the answer, God will come through for you if you don't give up!

Declare your Blessings in Advance

When we speak words of life and declare our blessings in advance, we are opening up ourselves to receive all that God has in store to give us. We can only do this from a heart that has the faith to believe for it, and the Bible says that "every one of us is given a measure of faith" (Romans 12:3). Even if your faith begins small, the more and more you repeat your requests and remind God of His promises, the closer you will be to receiving your miracle. Over time, if you do not give up your faith will lead you to your reality (Galatians 6:9, Mark 10:27).

If you are sick and dealing with an illness and you desire to be healed, start by saying, "I am strong, I am healthy, I will live out my days in fullness and health. Father, You have promised to bring health and healing to me, prosperity, security, and abundance of life, and I know I can have what You say I can have" (Jeremiah 33:6). When you begin to declare God's blessing over your life you will begin to see changes. Start declaring God's promises of healing, blessings, and favor, and get in agreement with what He says about you. When you start to do this in advance, not only will your faith be strengthened but you are making strides towards your victory.

When I was in my early 20's I was invited to go jet skiing by a good friend of mine who always played things safe. I had never seen him yell at others, be disrespectful, or act crazy in any way, but on the day we went jet skiing he decided to act like a wild child! What I thought would be a fun and easy jet skiing ride along the lake turned into the scariest day ever.

My friend started going 80-100 miles per hour, swerving, jumping waves, and making sharp turns. I began to yell, "Slow down, slow down," but of course he didn't. While traveling faster than the speed of light, his jet ski capsized and we were thrown off with full force. When we finally came up from the water, we could not find where the jet ski went. Then, WHAM, the jet ski hit me right in the left side of my knee. My knee instantly blew up and became so swollen. I eventually was able to make it back to shore with help and my friend encouraged me to get to the doctor, but I told him I could still walk and it would be okay.

It finally did end up being okay, but over time the side of my left knee became sensitive to touch and I remember seeing a doctor in passing who stated, "Yeah, your knee may be fine now, but eventually you will most likely develop arthritis in that knee." That always registered in the back of my head.

As I got older, I could feel the pain and sensitivity increasing in my knee, which only seemed to get worse over time. The doctor's words often swirled around in my head and I knew the enemy used that spoken word to cause me to dwell on my problem. The more I dwelled on the pain, the worse it became. So instead, I decided to take action. When the enemy spoke up again to remind me of the problem, I spoke back and reminded him of God's promises over my life. I decided in my heart that I was not going to let the enemy have his way.

I decided to come into agreement with what God had said over my life and declared that I was healed and blessed in advance. The prayer that I prayed was:

"Lord, You know I did not ask for this to happen, nor did I do it on purpose, but even still, I know that You desire that I be healed. Your words say that it is Your will that I prosper, enjoy good health, even as my soul prospers (3 John 1:2). Everywhere you went you healed people of all their diseases; not some of them, but all their diseases (Psalms 103:3). And Lord, You said in Your word, "Call upon me and I will answer you, and I will show you great and mighty things that you do not know" (Jeremiah 33:3). I call upon Your name now, Lord, and I ask that You heal me as You also desire that I be healed. My healing makes You smile, and this is something that I want as well. I ask this in Your precious name, Jesus, and I thank You for the answer in advance."

Each and every day I started to declare God's blessings and promises over my life. When the pain would try to emerge I would quickly say, "No, God is restoring health unto me, He is healing every part of my knee that was damaged, and that area is being reconstructed and healed." We know that the Word of God is "alive, active, and sharper than any two-edged sword and it pierces into the separation of our soul and spirit, our joints and marrow and our bones" (Hebrews 4:12). When you speak God's words over any area of your body, it must obey.

The word of God and His promises are alive and active and can travel deep within the area that it needs to go into to get the result that is needed. That spoken word over my knee, with faith, is what brought my healing. As

I began to do this daily, I began to notice that the sensitivity and pain in my left knee began to disappear, which was not the case for so many years. I was and continue to remain healed. I smile now because I know God's word is powerful and most of all it works!

You also have the power to declare your blessings in advance. You can also use God's words to combat every area of your life that needs change. God is faithful to look over His word and He promises to perform it (Jeremiah 1:12). It is not God's desire for you to sit around hurting, discouraged, depressed, or in despair. No, His plan and will for you are to be joyful despite your circumstances (1 Thessalonians 5:16-18). The word of God teaches us to "be strong and of good courage, never give up, and fight for what you need" (Joshua 1:9). It is better to declare that you are healed

> We know "that all things work together for our good to those who love God, and to those that are called according to His purpose. (Romans 8:28).

and will come out of debt than sit around and say or do nothing at all.

It is all about your faith in God and His promises and your desire to see a change in your life. You must go after the thing that you need with all your heart, mind, and soul. When you do this, God sees from heaven your desire, persistence, and determination and will move on your behalf by His will, and His will for you is always good. We know "that all things work together for our good to those who love God, and to those that are called according to His purpose. (Romans 8:28). God has great plans for you. Start declaring His plans and promises over your life in advance, believe His word, and expect great things!

I Am Who God Says I Am

The Israelites were getting invaded. After planting their crops and awaiting their harvest and the reward of their hard work, the Midianites came in droves and stripped them of all their crops, livestock, and everything they owned, leaving them to starve to death. The Israelites who were God's people began to cry out to God for help, and God heard their plea. (Judges 6)

God wanted to save His people and looked around for a man that He could use, and He found the one He wanted. An angel of God came down and said to Gideon, "Mighty hero, the Lord is with you!" (Judges 6:12) However, Gideon was a man that came from an undistinguished background that he considered to be weak and of a lower class. When God called him "Mighty hero" I'm sure Gideon looked around him and thought, "Are you talking to me?" He was shocked and surprised that God would say such a thing about him, especially when he felt quite the opposite. The angel then began to tell Gideon that God wanted to use him to save the Israelites.

When Gideon heard this he must have been shaking in his boots. "Me? You want to use me? Why me? How can I rescue the Israelites? My tribe is the weakest in our whole land, and on top of that, I am at the bottom of the list in my family" (see Judges 6).

Gideon was giving God all the reasons why he would not qualify for the job and why he could not do what God was asking of him. He felt inadequate to complete the assignment God was asking him to do, but God saw what Gideon could not see. God said, "Even though you call yourself weak, I call you mighty. Even though you call

202

yourself less than, I call you more than. Even though you say, 'I am not worthy,' I say you are worthy. Even though you say, 'I cannot do it,' I say you can. Yes, I believe in you and I will use you despite your weakness to shame the strong" (1 Corinthians 1:27).

This is what God says about you. When you do not feel that you qualify or have the ability to accomplish your dreams, God is saying that He has given you everything you need to do the very thing He has put into your heart. Gideon did not feel like a mighty warrior. Instead, he was insecure, nervous, and fearful of the task God was asking him to do. He did not feel equipped nor ready for what was being asked of him. However, the Lord turned to him and said, "Go with the strength you have, and rescue Israel from the Midianites. I am sending you!"

Wow, this is pretty amazing! Despite Gideon's spoken list of all the reasons why he *could not* do something, God still used him. God did not tell him that he needed to muster up more strength and be something that he was not. Instead, God told him to go with the "strength he already had" (Judges 6:14). In other words, God was saying, "You have everything you need to get the job done. You are not short of anything. Instead, you have all that it takes within you to accomplish what I am asking you to do. I did not make a mistake when I chose you and it's you that I have chosen to complete this assignment."

It is interesting to know that God chose Moses, David, and Gideon, all who were at the bottom of the lists in their families or felt inadequate in some way to do great things. God was able to use their weaknesses and insecurities to show forth His power and strength. The Bible says, "God chose the things the world considers foolish to shame those who think they are wise. He also chose things that are powerless or weak to shame those that are powerful or strong" (1 Corinthians 1:27). When we are weak and need to rely on the Lord for His help, God will get the glory. On the flip side, if we are strong and do not necessarily need to rely on God as much, then our pride rises and we do not end up giving God all the glory.

God used Gideon, and despite his shortcomings, He prophesied that he was a mighty and a victorious hero. In the same way, God believes and says the same about you! He says, "You are strong, and more than a conqueror, you are smart, well-equipped for the job, and ready to accomplish the task He has set before you!" God has given you talents, skills, gifts, and abilities, not just for yourself, but so you can be a light in the world and give Him all the glory.

Don't say the opposite of what God says about you in His word. He wants you to speak forth life from your mouth and say what He says about you. God wants you to say, "I can do all things through Christ who strengthens me. I am victorious, I can accomplish everything I need to do. I am worthy

> I can do all things through Christ who strengthens me (Philippians 4:13)

to receive good things from God. I am loved and I know that Jesus loves me." God wants you to say good things about yourself, because that's what He says about you.

Rather than making a list of all the reasons why you will not be able to complete the assignment as Gideon did, instead make a list of all the reasons why you *can* complete the task that God has in store for you. Even though Gideon needed a little reassurance from God, he had decided to put his fears behind him. Little by little, he took one step at a time toward the task that was given to him until he was able to win the battle and defeat Israel's enemies. The Lord was with Gideon, He never left his side, just as He will never leave your side. Will you trust Him? Will you hold on to God's promises that He has spoken over you to do all that He has created you to do? If you said yes, then you are on your way to do amazing things and accomplish the dreams, desires, and purposes that He has put within you.

Expect Your Miracle

Prayer is a way that we can communicate our thoughts, feelings, and our heart with God's heart. Our words have the power and potential to reach the Creator of the Universe. With your words you are able to call forth your healing, your deliverance, and your provision. When you and I pray, we ought to expect that God will move on our behalf and we will receive the things for which we pray.

The Bible says, "This is the confidence that we have before Him, that if we *ask* anything according to His will, He hears us, and if we know that He hears us then we know that we already *possess* what we have asked of Him" (1 John 5:15). You and I have the power and authority to come boldly before the Throne of Grace and ask for what we need, and God is gracious and loving enough to answer our needs. When you call on God to meet a need in your life, you must believe and expect great things!

Often people pray for things but do not expect to receive an answer. However, this is not what God wants for us.

God wants us to, ask, believe, pray, and expect that He will move on our behalf. When we expect something, it means that we look for it, we keep our eyes open, and we look around us knowing that God is going to meet us some way, somehow. In order to expect the answer to your prayer you must have faith, and faith will grow as you continue to hear the word of God and get His promises down on the inside of you (Romans 10:17).

This is what Elijah did when he prayed for rain. The Israelites turned away from God under the direction of an evil king named Ahab. Ahab disobeyed God by turning from Him and leading the Israelites in worshiping an idol named Baal. God told Elijah to send a word to Ahab that there would not be any rain or even a drop of dew for three years as a result of King Ahab and Israel's sin and disobedience. The rain stopped, the plants withered, and the streams dried up, causing a drought in the land. God eventually made it clear to both King Ahab and the Israelites that He alone was the Creator of the universe and Master over heaven and earth. The people cried out in repentance and asked for forgiveness for their mistakes. They used their voices to lift a cry up to heaven so that God would help them, and He did.

Elijah, with the spirit of God, told the people that it was going to rain. He then went to seek God for the answer to his prayer. He climbed to the top of Mount Carmel, bowed low to the ground, and prayed with his face in between his knees. He was asking God to answer his prayer for rain. He then told his servant, "Go and look out toward the sea." The servant went and looked, and said, "I do not see anything." Elijah then told him to look six more times. Finally, on the seventh time, his servant told him, "I see a little cloud about the size of a man's hand rising from the sea." Elijah knew what this meant and told his servant to go tell King Ahab the rain was coming! (1 Kings 18:44).

This is an illustration that when we pray, we ought to look for and expect an answer to our prayers. Your words have the power to create a change in your circumstances. Elijah was a great man of God and could have easily become discouraged because he did not see rain on the first, second, third, or fourth time. Instead, his prayers to God became more and more fervent and he continued looking for the answer even though his answers did not come immediately.

Even though the servant continued to come back with the report that "your prayers do not seem to be working, it does not look like it's going to happen," Elijah did not give up. He girded his loins, dug his feet into the ground, and was focused on receiving what he was asking of the Lord. He needed a miracle from God and was determined to get it! I honestly believe that Elijah would have waited there all day if he had to. He would have waited until he saw the hand of God move on his behalf. When he prayed, he believed that God would answer him, and because of his faith and expectation, he received the answer to his prayers. The rain came in torrents upon the land. He expected God to do a miracle and God did.

> God has promised to meet all your needs according to the riches of His glory in Christ Jesus and He will do what He has promised! [1]

Jesus also wants to answer your prayers, and sometimes you may need to earnestly seek and go after the answer to your prayers until you receive them (Colossians 4:2, James 5:16). Elijah continued to pray until he received what he was asking of God. He believed that he would receive an answer and he got it. The next time you sit down to pray, ask God for your needs and then go ahead and start praising and thanking God for the answer in advance (Mark 11:24). God has promised to meet all your needs according to the riches of His glory in Christ Jesus and He will do what He has promised! [1]

CHAPTER 16

There is Nothing Like the Word of God

The Bible is the *word* of God and there is incredible power that is available to those who adhere to it. It does not get any better than that! It is the most important guide to show us how we can live the best life now. Often people think it's just a book of rules, of do's and dont's, but it truly is just the opposite. The word of God is not given to us to make our lives miserable but to make it so much better.

What I have learned is that God's intent in giving us the word is to protect us, help encourage us, uplift us when we are down, and give us hope. When we take time to read God's word, we are giving God the authority to help change us from the inside out. When our inner man begins to change, our attitude and the words which we speak begin to change as well. The Word of God offers us advice and instruction on the best way to live our lives.

The book of Psalms speaks of God's faithfulness and goodness to us. Proverbs offers us wisdom and direction when we need help figuring out what the best plans for our lives would be.

Job teaches us what "not" to say to someone who is hurting and Corinthians tells us of God's love for us. There may have been times when someone has used their words to belittle you, discourage you, criticize, gossip, or talk ill of you; however, you are not alone.

Jesus Himself suffered many of the things that we have faced in our lives. He was criticized and gossiped about, He was betrayed and accused although He was innocent, and He was beaten unjustly. Joseph did all the right things, yet all the wrong things kept happening to him. He was lied about and became the center of gossip in his home. Joseph lost his childhood and had to quickly become an adult, yet God showered him with favor throughout the way. In the end what the enemy meant for evil, God turned for good. God caused Joseph to have favor and gave him a position of power and influence, and God restored Job to double.

Throughout the Bible, we can see story after story of people who have gone through similar situations to ours. Yet, in the end, these very same people remained faithful and continued to trust God in the midst of their circumstances. I used to think that reading the whole Bible was for old people, but I quickly realized after making several mistakes of my own that the Bible was there all along to keep me out of trouble, and to give me the best life that I can have. Now I read the word of God line by line, meditate on it, and always try to apply it to my life.

I remember having a conversation with a family member who seemed to struggle with a lot of relationship issues. She would say things like, "I have prayed and asked God for the right one, yet it does not seem to work out for me. I finally then meet this guy and he seemed so amazing! He was not a strong Christian like I am, but I really liked him! I don't understand why our relationship ended! I don't understand why God would allow this to happen to me!"

What my beautiful family member did not know was that God never intended for her to be with him in the first place. By spending time in God's word, we begin to understand the type of spouse God has described for us to have (see 2 Corinthians 6:14). The Bible even goes as far as to explain what we are to look for and talks to us about getting the advice of counselors before making any big decisions (Proverbs 11:14).

When we take time to read the owner's manual - which is the word of God - it helps show us which direction to go in, and warns us of the dangerous roads ahead. When we read scripture, over time it will become ingrained in our spirit. By doing this we allow the Holy Spirit to live within us, whose purpose is to comfort, teach, protect, and be our trustworthy guide. Jesus says in John 14:26 (AMP), "But the helper (counselor, advocate) and Holy Spirit, whom the Father will send in His name, will teach you all things."

> God's written word has the power to transform your life

Reading God's word daily will begin to change you from the inside out. You may find that the people around you will notice more of a difference in you as you continually feed your spirit. What's on the inside of you will eventually come out of you. This is often displayed in the way that we act, talk, and behave. Jesus loves you and died that you may live life to the fullest and his promises will become real to you as you continue to walk with him on a day-to-day basis. The closer you walk with Christ, the more quickly you will be able to hear His voice when He speaks to you. I encourage you to read God's word daily, listen to what God says to you through His written word and watch how it will transform your life!

God's Great Love

God's word is like a soothing balm. It calms our spirits and our hearts when we feel troubled. There have been many times in my life where I have felt troubled, whether it be over exams, friendships, marriage, children, or work. Life may not always be easy; however, God has promised to be with you, and comfort you in the process. John 16:33 says, "I have told you these things so that in Me you may have peace. In the world you will have tribulation, but take courage; I have overcome the world!" We are not exempt from trials, but we can be sure that when we face them, God is with us and has promised to never leave nor forsake us (Hebrews 13:5).

> *God is with us and has promised to never leave nor forsake us (Hebrews 13:5).*

The Lord not only provides peace, but also He provides us strength, courage, and the ability to move forward. I heard a story of a woman who was losing her son to drugs, alcohol, and a life of homosexuality. In addition to this heartbreak, her marriage was falling apart and she eventually came to a point of considering suicide. During her time of despair, someone passed a tract and told her about Jesus. She ended up finding out about the love of Jesus and started to explore her own identity in Christ.

Her son, being born from Chinese immigrants, never felt like he fit in at school or in the American culture. As a child, he was introduced to pornography from a very young age through his neighborhood friends. After some time, he noticed that he started to become attracted to both men and women and his passion for men began to grow stronger. He then began to feel that he was homosexual and his life took on a spiral of sin, multiple sexual encounters, and drugs that led him to jail.

This young man's parents were mortified by his behavior, but his parents never gave up on praying. His mother, especially, began to press into God, pray fervently, and fight for her son's life. She cried out to God daily to help keep her son from living a life of sin and to be set free from his homosexual lifestyle and addictions. Then one day, unexpectedly, her son was caught by the police for drug possession and he was sent to jail. His situation seemed more hopeless than ever before, but he then took a turn for the worse. He was told by the county jail nurse that he was HIV+. His body was in shock and he felt hopeless, yet God did not give up on him! He found a Bible in a trash can within his jail cell and began to read it fervently.

It was then that he realized that God never meant for him to live a life of sin, but to live a life that honored Christ. After years of his parent's tears, prayers, and a fight for life, he realized that he no longer had to focus on his

213

sexual identity, but now rather focuses on his identity in Christ. This young man who was once a prodigal son had been set free from a life of sin, and now has a strong relationship with Christ and lives a life that honors God. [1] God's word convicts and corrects us, and helps to lead us on a path that offers us peace, love, and joy when we come into agreement with His plans for us.

When I read the Bible and spend time meditating on the word, I see God's love for all of humanity. Jesus loved you and I enough to die for us on the cross, so we would have eternal life and one day be with Him in glory. He became the ultimate sacrifice for every one of us, and His word begins to show us His great plan for our lives and His deep love for us.

In Ephesians 3:18, Paul says, "I pray that you may have the power to understand, as all God's people should, how wide, how long, how high, and how deep His love is for you. May you experience the love of Christ, though it is too great to fully understand. Then you will be made complete with all the fullness of life and power that comes from God." Jesus loves you and me more than we can ever imagine, and the Bible says that nothing can ever separate us from the love of God.

Neither death nor life, neither angels nor demons, neither our fears for today nor our worries about tomorrow, not even the powers of hell can separate us from God's love. There is no power in the sky above or in the earth below; indeed, nothing in all creation will ever be able to separate us from the love of God that is revealed in Christ Jesus our Lord" (see Romans 8:38-39).

God is saying, "My love for you is never changing, there is nothing you could have done, nor will do, that can keep me from loving you. You are my prize possession, I created you in your mother's womb and I have a plan for your life. These plans are to prosper you and not to harm you, rather they are to give you hope and a future" (Jeremiah 29:11). You are a child of the Most High King, and His very *words to you* are to show you His great and everlasting love for you that is unchanging.

A Daily Walk

Storing God's word in your heart will change you from within, and that change will come out through the words of your mouth and can be seen in your character. We ought to store God's word in us when we don't need it so that it will come out of us when we do need it. The only way to place God's word within our hearts is to have a daily walk with Him.

Once you accept Jesus Christ as your savior, it is so important to spend time with Him. Spending time with God helps us to grow in our faith while helping us to understand who He is and His great love for us. Often. I run into new believers who say, "I know that Jesus is real, but I don't know what to do next. I have never been taught to read the Bible and pray so I am not sure what I am supposed to do from here." I simply tell them, "It just starts by taking it one day at a time and creating a habit or a routine that starts at the same time every day. It's kind of like waking up and making a cup of coffee. You do not forget the coffee because it's now a part of your routine."

God's word tells us that Jesus woke up early to pray. Mark 1:35 says, "Very early in the morning, while it was still dark, Jesus got up, and went off to a solitary place, where He prayed." Not only did He do this, but Abraham and David also woke up early to spend time in God's presence. David said, "My voice shalt thou hear in the morning, O LORD, in the morning will I direct my prayer unto Thee and I wait expectantly." (Psalms 5:3).

Setting our face towards God in the morning can often be the best time in the day to start reading God's word, to pray, and spend time in His presence. When we pray in the morning, it prepares our heart for the day ahead and is often the only time that it is quiet. This time allows us to quiet our hearts before God, talk to Him, and listen while allowing God to speak back to us. Prayer gives us strength; it allows us to cry out to the Lord and get everything off our chest. It also lets us know that the Creator of the universe "has heard us, and if we know that He has heard us, then we will know that we will have what we have asked of Him" (John 5:15).

There have been many times in my life that I have needed to get on my knees and cry out to the Lord. Spending time in God's presence allows me to unload all of my burdens on to Him. The Bible says, "Cast your care upon him, for He cares for you" (1 Peter 5:7). Jesus cares for us and does not want us to feel like we have to carry all of our burdens ourselves. Instead, He says, "Come to me, all who are weary or heavy laden, and I will give you rest [easy, light, refreshing for your soul]. Take my yoke upon you, and learn from Me, for I am gentle and lowly in heart, and you will find rest for

> "Cast your care upon him, for He cares for you" (1 Peter 5:7).

your souls. For My yoke is easy, and My burden is light" (Matthew 11:28-30 (AMPC).

God has promised to be with both you and I and carry the things that we cannot carry. He says that the burdens or tests that we have will never be too much for us to bear, but with His help and strength, we will get through it when we come to Him (1 Corinthians 10:13). When you have troubles and opposition that the enemy places on you, run to God for the answer. The Bible says that "there is an enemy of our soul who also has come to steal, kill, and destroy. Rather, our God is love and He has come to give us good things." [1] Praying and spending time with God does not come naturally for some, but it is so necessary to cultivate a relationship with God and draw closer to Him.

My 9-year-old son is now learning this process. He was so used to me praying for him daily and asking God for his protection that he had not learned to develop his own relationship with Christ. So, as a parent, I felt that I needed to make some changes. I told my young son that I was going to buy him an alarm clock. I would then set the timer at least 10 minutes before he gets out of bed to spend time with God. At first, he argued, fussed, and cried because this was not easy on his flesh, but I knew it would strengthen his soul and spirit. He now actually looks forward to his time with God, enjoys it, and practices this process daily.

The more we develop this habit and practice it daily, the easier it will become. Spending time in God's court begins by making a decision that places God as the highest priority of our day. When we keep God first, our days will go smoother and we will be able to handle situations better than we expected. When we put God's word within us daily, we allow the Holy Spirit to help us in times of hardship, opposition, or troubles. God will send the Holy Spirit to remind you of verses in the Bible that will guide or direct you, which is God's way of speaking to you.

The word of God is the primary way that God communicates and talks to us, and that is why it is so important to store His instructions within our hearts. When you walk and talk with God on a daily basis, your life will begin to change in ways that you never expected. You will begin to act, talk, and imitate the way He lived his life, and that change will be seen by those that surround you. Decide to walk with God daily and when you do this, your life will change dramatically.

Jesus Loves You

Jesus loves you, more than you will ever know. He died on the cross for the sins of the world and has given us mercy and grace even when we did not deserve it. There is no mistake that you and I could ever make that would separate us from His love. Even if you go to the highest mountain or dip into the lowest sea, He is there with you (Psalms 139).

God made you in His very own image and created your innermost being while knitting you together in your mother's womb. [1] He never made a mistake when He created you because you are fearfully and wonderfully made. [2] His thoughts toward you are good, and He sees every tear that you have cried and knows every hair on your head. [3] He knows more about you than anyone else could ever know, and even still He says, " I love you." [4] There is no mistake so great, or a sin that you have committed that is beyond comprehension that can keep His love away from you, and He loves you too much to let you go. Displayed in the Bible are God's words to us. He tells us how much He loves us in great detail. Sometimes we don't even realize how much He cares for us, but He does. Christ has written a love letter to you through His written word and this is what He says....

Jesus Says to You:

"You are my child and I am your Father. I am your everlasting Father and I will guide you in the paths that you should take. [5] *I am the Father that comforts you. Whether you turn to the right or to the left, I will be there. Your ears will hear Me saying behind you, "This is the way - walk in it" (Isaiah 30:21). It was never My plan for you to hurt in any way, nor be discouraged, rather run to Me and I will keep you safe.* [6] *When you go through tough times, I will be there for you. I will be a refuge, a strong tower that gives you strength in your time of need.* [7]

You see, I want to give you good things and do more for you than you can ever imagine, dream, or think by the very power that is within you. [8] *I put the sun, moon, and stars in their place, is there anything too hard for me? (Genesis 18:14). When you were broken-hearted, I came close to you, and I have promised to heal your broken heart and bind up your wounds.* [9] *My love for you has always been the same, and I want to do a new thing in your life, do you know it, can you perceive it? For I can even make a road in the wilderness and rivers in the deserts for you (Isaiah 43:19). I do this for you because you are My child and I love you."*

If you seek Me with all your heart you will find Me, and there I will outstretch My hand toward you and comfort you. [10] *I am yours and you are Mine, and before the world was created, I chose you and ordained you and I have a wonderful plan ahead for you.* [11] *You see, I am the one who has placed those desires within you, and I delight to give you the desires of your heart. (Psalms 37:4). Will you believe and ask Me for what you need?* [12] *For My plans for you are good and not to harm you, but to give you hope and a future. (Jeremiah 29:11)*

I want you to know that I will never leave you nor forsake you because you are engraved in the palm of My hands, and your walls are continually before Me. [13] *You are My precious child, a masterpiece that I call My own.* [14] *I will protect and guide you in the day of trouble and I will have my angels surround you in whichever way you go.* [14] *I will put a shield around you that your enemies cannot penetrate and My righteous right hand will uphold you. These are My words to you because you are My precious child. I love you and have wonderful plans for you, reach out to Me and I will wrap you in My loving arms. For you are loved, you are Mine, and you will forever be in My heart.*

Love,
Your Heavenly Father

You Can Make a Change

God's words toward us are to encourage us, enlighten us, and give us life more abundantly. He wants you to use your words for good and not for evil, to give life and offer hope to the many that surround you, each and every day.

In return, you will find a new sense of joy, peace, and satisfaction. You may never know, but your small word of encouragement, agreement, love, and kindness can touch the heart of those that may be hurting within.

God can use you to be a catalyst for change within your home, within your school, and your workplace. Will you allow God to use you? If so, you will begin to see changes within your life, and the lives of others, that will ultimately affect your future. You and I have a choice every day to create change within our atmosphere. Remember, if given an opportunity to speak life or death in a person's life: Choose life!

AFTERWORD

I pray that this book has been a blessing to you and has ministered to you in the areas that you have needed it the most. God wants great things for you and His way is always the very best way. If you are like me and have made mistakes along the way in life, you are not alone! None of us are perfect, but we can all make strides to living a more abundant life that God wants to give us. You can change your life and your future one word at a time. Jesus loves you and desires that you walk in victory. Trust God to help make the changes in the areas you need the most and He will lead you on the right path. Let me take a moment now and speak a blessing over you!

Father, I ask, in Your precious name, that you will bless your son or daughter today. I ask that your Holy Spirit guide them, protect them, and lead them on the path they are to take. I speak Your greatest blessings over Your child's life and pray for Your unconditional love and peace to surround them and fill their hearts with Your presence and love. May Your grace and spirit always be with them, and may Your presence live forever in their hearts, both now and until eternity, and in Jesus' name I pray. AMEN!

Would You Like to Have a Relationship With Jesus Christ?

Jesus loves you and He has a great plan for your life. He has a unique and specific plan just for you, and wants to do great things in and through you. No matter what you have done, where you have gone, or how many mistakes you have made, God's grace and love is greater than your sin.

Jesus died on the cross for you, to lovingly offer you forgiveness and mercy and give you a brand-new life in Him. He has been waiting for you to ask Him into your heart, so that He can be your Lord and Savior. If you have never made Jesus the Lord of your life and asked Him for forgiveness of your past mistakes and sins, I want to invite you to do so.

Let's begin with saying this prayer...

Lord Jesus, thank You for dying on the cross for my sins and forgiving me of everything I have done wrong. I know that I need You and I cannot live without You. I believe You died on the cross for my sins so that I can have a new life in You. I confess with my mouth and believe in my heart that You are the Lord and Savior of my life. I ask that You take me just as I am and clean out all the areas of my life that do not please you. I want to live for You from now on until I see You again. I am so thankful that You have given me another chance and a fresh new start to live a life that serves and honors You.

I love You, and I thank You for all that You have done for me!

Congratulations! If you have decided to make Jesus Christ the Lord of your life, you are on your way to living a life full of victory! Jesus wants to have a personal relationship with you and wants to spend time with you each and every day. I want to encourage you to spend some time to read God's word and pray daily. When you do this, your spirit will become full of God's love and He will use you in great and awesome ways. I also encourage you to find a Bible-based church that you can grow in, and fill your life with all the good things God has in store for you.

May God Bless you!

Acknowledgments

First and foremost I would like to thank God for the support and strength he has given me to be able to write and finish this book. Without him, this book would not have been a possibility.

To my mom, thank you for all the love and support you have shown me and " just being there" to help and support me along the way. I will never forget you for that!

To my son Jayden (age 9), who helped to edit my book with "your little eyes", to make it that much better for my readers.

To my friend and author Pantea Kalhor, for all your help and support in making this book possible.

To my Dad, who sparked the desire within me to write a book and encouraged me to keep going.

To my Husband, who always pushed me forward and believed in me, for that I am grateful.

To those who are reading this book, I want to acknowledge you, and say thank you for making this book possible. Your support in purchasing and spreading the word of this book will help people throughout the world. I pray God's greatest blessings upon you and thank you once again.

Let's Connect

Dear Reader, If this book has been helpful to you. Please feel free to *leave me a review* on Amazon. I would love to hear from you! I also pray God's greatest blessings on your life, and I believe God is going to do great things in and through you.

I'd love to hear your story and how my book has helped you. You can connect with me through:

https://www.subscribepage.com/i4o3k7

Notes

Chapter 1

[1] Colossians 4:6, Titus 3:1-2.

[2] Genesis 50:20

[3] John 29:11

[4] James 3:3

[5] Colossians 4:6

Be Careful What You Say

[1] See Numbers 12

[2] John 15:15

[3] Proverbs 16:33

[4] Proverbs 18:21

[5] Matthew 5:14

Chapter 2

Don't Dig Up your Seeds

[1] Luke 11:9

[2] 1 Kings 18:44

[3] James 1:6-7

[4] Psalm 37:4

Chapter 4

Learning the Hard Way

[1] Job 12:12; Exodus 20:12

[2] Proverbs 3:7, Proverbs 12:15

[3] Proverbs 19:27

Sights, Sounds and Surroundings:

[1] (1 Corinthians 15:33 (NIV

[2] (2 Corinthians 6:14 (NIV)

Chapter 5

Guard your mouth

[1] Got Questions- Your Questions, Biblical Answers (2019, July 26). *What are idle words?* Retrieved from: https://www.gotquestions.org/idle-words.html

[2] Psalm 141:3, Proverbs 21:23

[3] Luke 6: 27-28

[4] Ephesians 4:29

Where the Mind goes the mouth follows

[1] Philippians 4:8-9

Take every thought captive

[1] James 4:7

[2] Philippians 4:6-9

[3] Luke 10:19

Chapter 6

Who do you say you are?

[1] Matthew 12:33-35

[2] Proverbs 17:27-28

Put on the Full Armor of God

[1] 3 John 1:2

[2] Psalms 37:5

The Word that Fell on Stony ground

[1] John 10:10

Chapter 7

Idle Words

[1] Miriam-Webster Dictionary-idle. 2019. In *Merriam-Webster.com*.Retrieved September 29, 2019, from https://www.merriam-webster.com/dictionary/idle

[2] 2 Timothy 2:16

Keep the Peace

[1] Proverbs 14:29, Proverbs 19:1

[2] John 10:10

Chapter 8

God's Ears are Open to our Prayers

[1] Romans 12:19

[2] Luke 6:45

[3] Joel 2:25

[4] Matthew 12:35

Avoiding Verbal Pitfalls

[1] James 4:17

[2] https://www.goodreads.com/quotes/833766-it-is-the-holy-spirit-s-job-to-convict-god-s-job

[3] Proverbs 13:3 &Proverbs 10:19

[4] Jeremiah 29:11

Think and Talk about Good Things

[1] Daystar (2016). *Dodie Osteen: Trust, Fear and the Everlasting Love of Jesus.* Retrieved from https://www.daystar.com/news-updates/general-updates/dodie-osteen-trust-fear-and-the-everlasting-love-of-jesus/

[2] James 1:19

Chapter 9

Change your perspective

[1] Roget's 21st Century Thesaurus Philip Leaf Group (3rd ed). (2013). Thesaurus*.com*. Retrieved September 29, 2019, from https://www.thesaurus.com/browse/perspective

[2] My Perspectives Committed to Inspire (retrieved-2019). *A Tale of Two Shoe Salesman* Retrieved from https://myprespectives.wordpress.com/2012/06/24/a-tale-of-two-shoe-salesmen/

As a man thinketh

[1] Deuteronomy 28:13

[2] Philippians 4:13

Romans 8:31

Chapter 10

[1] 2 Corinthians 5:17

[2] Deuteronomy 28:6

[3] Hebrews 10:17

[4] Romans 15:7, John 3:3-8

[5] Jeremiah 1, Exod. 33:12; Isa. 49:1, 5; Rom. 8:29

Chapter 11

[1] Luke 12:12

Chapter 12

Speak words that Heal

[1] Isaiah 43:2

[2] I Thessalonians 5:16-18

Words of Love

[1] Corinthians 13:4-8

Words of Affirmation

[1] Proverbs 11:25-31

Healing for Body, Mind, Soul and Spirit

[1] 1 Thessalonians 5: 17-18

Chapter 13

Speak it into Existence

[1] John 10:10

[2] Ephesians 6:12

What do you Say?

[1] Genesis 1:27

[2] Philippians 4:13

Chapter 14

A Joyful Heart

[1] Wikipedia contributors. (2019, September 30). *Diamond (gemstone).* In Wikipedia: The Free Encyclopedia. Retrieved August 20,2019 from: https://en.wikipedia.org/wiki/Diamond_(gemstone)

Chapter 15

Prophesying your future

[1] Otabil, M. (2019, September 15). *Prophecy Quote.* Retrieved from https://www.allchristianquotes.org/quotes/Pastor_Mensa_Otabil/7017/

[2] Joel 3:10

Expect a Miracle

[1] Philippians 4:19

Chapter 16

Your Great Love

[1] Medium Publishous: (n.d.) *Out of a far Country.* Retrieved from https://medium.com/publishous/6-real-life-prodigal-stories-to-encourage-you-and-strengthen-your-faith-898dab439310

A Daily walk

[1] 1 John 4:8

Jesus Loves You

[1] Genesis 1:27

[2] Psalms 139:14

[3] Luke 12:7

[4] Psalms 56:8

[5] Psalms 32:8

[6] Proverbs 18:20

[7] Psalms 46 1-3, Proverbs 18:10.

[8] Ephesians 3:20.

[9] Psalms 34:18, Psalms 147:3.

[10] Deuteronomy 4:29.

[11] John 15:16. Leviticus 20:26, Isaiah 43:1,

[12] Matthew 21:22

[13] Hebrews 13:5, Isaiah 49:16.

[14] Isaiah 43: 1&4, Ephesians 2:10

[15] Psalms 50:15, Exodus 23:20

[16] Isaiah 41:10, Psalms 3:3. Deuteronomy 31:6

About the Author

Julie Thomas is an author a leader, singer and a teacher of God's word. She is a woman that is very passionate about Christ and is filled with energy, love and a deep desire to help and encourage those around her. She lives in the Florida area with her two beautiful boys and enjoys adventure, travel, spending time with family and so much more.

Her heart is to uplift, and inspire people of all ages, nationalities and backgrounds. She also has a desire to teach you what God has taught her over the years and believes if God can transform her life he can do the same for you!

Made in the USA
Middletown, DE
28 May 2021